UPGRADE

Organizadora:

Richmond Educação
Obra coletiva concebida, desenvolvida e
produzida pela Richmond Educação.

Editora Responsável:

Gisele Aga
Licenciada em Letras Português/Inglês pelas
Faculdades Metropolitanas Unidas.

Professora em escolas particulares e cursos
de idiomas em São Paulo há 16 anos.

Coordenadora pedagógico-comercial
em cursos de idiomas há 6 anos.

Editora.

VOLUME

2

COMPONENTE CURRICULAR:
LÍNGUA ESTRANGEIRA MODERNA – INGLÊS

1ª edição
São Paulo, 2010

Richmond

Elaboração dos originais

Ana Rosa Marinho Oliveira Vivarini
Licenciada em Letras pela Faculdade da Região dos Lagos.
Professora de inglês em escolas particulares em Cabo Frio há 19 anos.

Carla Maurício Coelho da Silva Vianna
Bacharel em Letras pela Universidade Federal do Rio de Janeiro.
Professora em escolas particulares e públicas há 15 anos.
Coordenadora pedagógico-administrativa em cursos de idiomas há 6 anos.

Claudia Priore
Licenciada em Letras pela Universidade Paulista.
Professora em escolas particulares em São Paulo há 16 anos.

Daniella Bergamo
Bacharel em Letras com habilitação em Tradutor e Intérprete pela Faculdade Ibero-Americana de Letras e Ciências Humanas.
Professora e Coordenadora de Área por 6 anos.
Professora de Língua Inglesa por 14 anos.
Professora de Língua Portuguesa para estrangeiros por 12 anos.

Gisele Aga
Licenciada em Letras (Português/Inglês) pelas Faculdades Metropolitanas Unidas.
Professora em escolas particulares e cursos de idiomas em São Paulo há 16 anos.
Coordenadora pedagógico-comercial em cursos de idiomas há 6 anos.
Editora.

Heloisa Helena Soares Quirino
Bacharel em Português/Inglês pela Faculdade de Humanidades Pedro II.
Professora de inglês em escolas particulares há 23 anos.

Izaura Valverde
Bacharel em Letras com habilitação em Português e Inglês, pela Universidade Mackenzie.
Licenciada em Letras com habilitação em Português e Inglês, pela Universidade Mackenzie.
Professora de inglês há 24 anos.
Coordenadora da área de inglês em escolas particulares em São Paulo há 11 anos.
Autora de livros didáticos.

João Rodrigo Lima Agildo
Bacharel em Letras pela Universidade de São Paulo.
Professor de inglês em escolas particulares em São Paulo há 11 anos.

Luciana Silva
Mestre em Letras, área de concentração: Linguística Aplicada, pela Universidade Federal de Minas Gerais.
Professora de inglês há 22 anos.
Professora do Centro Pedagógico da Universidade Federal de Minas Gerais há 3 anos.

Luciana S. Pinheiro
Mestre em Letras e Cultura Regional pela Universidade Caxias do Sul.
Professora em escolas particulares, no PLE da Universidade de Caxias do Sul e Professora Formadora PROLIC/REGESD/UCS há 10 anos.
Assessora pedagógica a professores de escolas públicas e particulares.

Marcelo Furlin
Mestre em Comunicação e Letras pela Universidade Mackenzie.
Professor assistente em cursos de graduação e de pós-graduação (presenciais e à distância) da Universidade Metodista de São Paulo.
Professor de língua inglesa em escolas de idiomas há 24 anos.
Assessor pedagógico em editoras e em instituições de ensino (redes privada e pública).

Título original: *UPGRADE*
© Richmond Educação 2010

Coordenação editorial: Sandra Cristina Possas
Edição de texto: Gisele Aga
Assistência editorial: Adriana Beatriz Saporito
Preparação de texto: Maria Estela de Alcantara
Projeto gráfico: Andreza Moreira
Capa: Andreza Moreira
Coordenação de produção gráfica: André Monteiro, Maria de Lourdes Rodrigues
Coordenação de arte: Christiane Borin
Edição de arte: Andreza Moreira
Editoração eletrônica: Aeroestudio
Coordenação de revisão: Adriana Cristina Bairrada, Elaine Cristina del Nero
Revisão: Ana Curci, Augusto de Salvo Russo, Rafael Gustavo Spigel
Coordenação de pesquisa iconográfica: Ana Lucia Soares
Pesquisa iconográfica: Felipe Campos, Glaucy Vulcano, Mariana Lima
As imagens identificadas com a sigla CID foram fornecidas pelo Centro de Informação e Documentação da Editora Moderna.
Coordenação de *bureau*: Américo Jesus
Tratamento de imagens: Fabio N. Precendo, Alexandre Petreca, Pix Art
Pré-impressão: Helio P. de Souza Filho, Marcio Hideyuki Kamoto
Coordenação de produção industrial: Wilson Aparecido Troque
Impressão e acabamento: São Francisco Gráfica e Editora

Dados Internacionais de Catalogação na Publicação (CIP)
(Câmara Brasileira do Livro, SP, Brasil)

Upgrade / obra coletiva concebida, desenvolvida e produzida pela Richmond Educação; editora Gisele Aga. — São Paulo: Richmond Educação, 2010.

"Componente curricular: língua estrangeira Moderna: inglês"
Obra em 3 v.

1. Inglês – Estudo e ensino I. Aga, Gisele.

10-02355   CDD-420.7

Índices para catálogo sistemático:
1. Inglês : Ensino médio   420.7

RICHMOND EDUCAÇÃO LTDA.
Rua Padre Adelino, 758 - sala 3 - Belenzinho
São Paulo - SP - Brasil - CEP 03303-904
Vendas e Atendimento: 0800 771 8181
Fax (0_ _11) 2790-1284
www.richmond.com.br
2013
Impresso no Brasil

1   3   5   7   9   10   8   6   4   2

Contents

What's in the World?

REUTERS / LATINSTOCK

INDRANIL MUKHERJEE / STRINGER / AFP / GETTY IMAGES

RAFAEL GENTILE

DAVID GROSSMAN / ALAMY / OTHER IMAGES

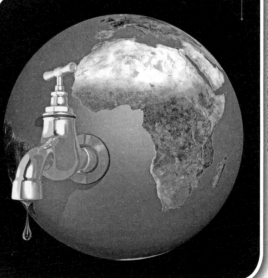

OLEKSIY MAKSYMENKO / ALAMY / OTHER IMAGES

Quiz

HOW MUCH DO YOU KNOW ABOUT THE WORLD?

1

How many kilos of beef do a Brazilian person and a Japanese person eat a year, respectively?

a ☐ 31.7 kg; 13.8 kg

b ☐ 56.3 kg; 31.7 kg

c ☐ 56.3 kg; 13.8 kg

d ☐ 13.8 kg; 31.7 kg

e ☐ 31.7 kg; 56.3 kg

2

Many native Brazilian plants are stolen by other countries for medical and financial purposes. Which country holds the most patents for Brazilian seeds?

a ☐ France

b ☐ United States of America

c ☐ Canada

d ☐ Germany

e ☐ Japan

3

The symbol below represents the social worker's job. What does it mean?

SERVIÇO SOCIAL

ILLUSTRATION: RAFAEL GENTILE

a ☐ It means justice for all.

b ☐ It means love and truth can overcome any difficulty.

c ☐ It means justice, ethics, and fairness in the job.

d ☐ It means morality and wellbeing are above everything.

e ☐ It means cordiality and fairness go a long way.

4

Can you guess who said the quotations below?

"As a nuclear power – as the only nuclear power to have used a nuclear weapon – the United States has a moral responsibility to act."

"As a rock star, I have two instincts; I want to have fun, and I want to change the world. I have a chance to do both."

a ☐ Bill Clinton and Bono Vox

b ☐ Bill Clinton and Justin Timberlake

c ☐ Bono Vox and Justin Timberlake

d ☐ Barack Obama and Justin Timberlake

e ☐ Barack Obama and Bono Vox

5

One of these writers is not Brazilian. Who is he?

a ☐ Pedro Bandeira

b ☐ Fernando Pessoa

c ☐ Manuel Bandeira

d ☐ Carlos Drummond de Andrade

e ☐ Monteiro Lobato

6

Publishers wanted to merchandise this cartoonist's work and they tried to force him to accept this. But he never changed his mind and never allowed the images of his creations to be used on mugs, stickers, or T-shirts. Who is this cartoonist?

a ☐ Scott Adams, creator of *Dilbert*.

b ☐ Bill Watterson, creator of *Calvin and Hobbes*.

c ☐ Jim Davis, creator of *Garfield*.

d ☐ Walt Disney, creator of *Donald Duck*.

e ☐ Matt Groening, creator of *The Simpsons*.

RAFAEL GENTILE

7

How much drinking water is used in the production of paper in Brazil?

a ☐ 200 to 750 liters/kg

b ☐ 300 to 900 liters/kg

c ☐ 500 to 1200 liters/kg

d ☐ 600 to 1900 liters/kg

e ☐ 750 to 2300 liters/kg

8

What is the most populous tribe in Brazil?

a ☐ Ianomâmi (AM and RR)

b ☐ Manaus (AM)

c ☐ Raposa Serra do Sol (RR)

d ☐ Alto Rio Negro (AM)

e ☐ Évare (AM)

1 We Are What We Eat

RAFAEL GENTILE

PRE-READING

Look at the title of the unit. What does it mean to you? Where can we find nutrition labels like the one below?

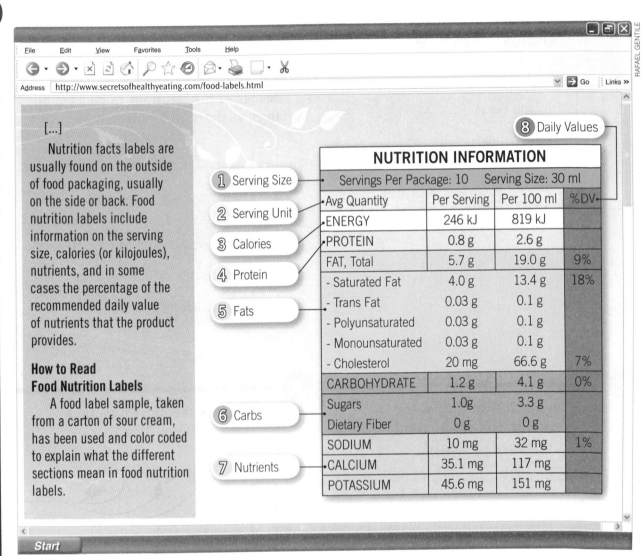

[...]

Nutrition facts labels are usually found on the outside of food packaging, usually on the side or back. Food nutrition labels include information on the serving size, calories (or kilojoules), nutrients, and in some cases the percentage of the recommended daily value of nutrients that the product provides.

How to Read Food Nutrition Labels

A food label sample, taken from a carton of sour cream, has been used and color coded to explain what the different sections mean in food nutrition labels.

1 Serving Size
2 Serving Unit
3 Calories
4 Protein
5 Fats
6 Carbs
7 Nutrients
8 Daily Values

NUTRITION INFORMATION

Servings Per Package: 10   Serving Size: 30 ml

Avg Quantity	Per Serving	Per 100 ml	%DV
ENERGY	246 kJ	819 kJ	
PROTEIN	0.8 g	2.6 g	
FAT, Total	5.7 g	19.0 g	9%
- Saturated Fat	4.0 g	13.4 g	18%
- Trans Fat	0.03 g	0.1 g	
- Polyunsaturated	0.03 g	0.1 g	
- Monounsaturated	0.03 g	0.1 g	
- Cholesterol	20 mg	66.6 g	7%
CARBOHYDRATE	1.2 g	4.1 g	0%
Sugars	1.0g	3.3 g	
Dietary Fiber	0 g	0 g	
SODIUM	10 mg	32 mg	1%
CALCIUM	35.1 mg	117 mg	
POTASSIUM	45.6 mg	151 mg	

Start

Extracted from <http://www.secretsofhealthyeating.com/food-labels.html>.
Accessed on October 22, 2009.

Avg (average) quantity: quantidade média
carton: caixa (de papelão ou de plástico)
coded: codificada
nutrition labels: rótulos nutricionais
packaging: embalagem
provides: fornece
sample: amostra
serving size: tamanho da porção
sour cream: creme de leite azedo, coalhada

After Reading

1 Go back to the text on page 8 and find six transparent words.

_____

_____

2 Look for the information below in the sour cream label sample.

a calories per serving   _____

b trans fat per serving   _____

c percentage of daily value of total fat   _____

d servings per package   _____

e dietary fiber   _____

3 Answer the questions.

a Where can you usually find the nutrition facts labels?

_____

b What information do the food nutrition labels include?

_____

_____

4 The following label is from an instant chocolate pudding dry mix. Compare this label to the one on page 8. Complete the sentences using the comparative forms of the adjectives in parentheses.

a The percentage of daily value of total fat in a serving of chocolate pudding mix isn't _____ (high) in a serving of sour cream.

b The chocolate pudding mix has more sugar and is _____ (sweet) the sour cream.

c The percentage of daily value of sodium in a serving of sour cream is _____ (low) in a serving of pudding mix.

d A serving of sour cream has _____ saturated fat _____ (more) a serving of chocolate pudding mix.

e A serving of pudding mix has _____ cholesterol _____ (less) a serving of sour cream.

Nutrition Facts

Serving Size 1 package 3.5 oz 99 g (99 g)
Servings per container 2

RAFAEL GENTILE

Amount Per Serving	
Calories 374	Calories from Fat 17

	% Daily Value*
Total Fat 2 g	3%
Saturated Fat 1 g	4%
Trans Fat	
Cholesterol 0 mg	0%
Sodium 1415 mg	59%
Total Carbohydrate 87 g	29%
Dietary Fiber 4 g	14%
Sugars 67 g	
Protein 2 g	

Vitamin A	0%	Vitamin C	0%
Calcium	1%	Iron	7%

* Percent Daily Values are based on a 2,000 calorie diet. Your daily values may be higher or lower depending on your calorie needs:

		Calories	2,000	2,500
Total Fat	Less than		65 g	80 g
Sat Fat	Less than		20 g	25 g
Cholesterol	Less than		300 mg	300 mg
Sodium	Less than		2,400 mg	2,400 mg
Total Carbohydrate			300 g	375 g
Fiber			25 g	30 g

Calories per gram:
Fat 9   •   Carbohydrate 4   •   Protein 4

www.NutritionData.com

Extracted from <http://www.nutritiondata.com>.
Accessed on January 10, 2010.

Vocabulary in Use

1 Find six adjectives in the word search below.

T	W	H	E	A	J	R	N	X
G	A	S	A	L	T	Y	I	G
U	T	Y	Q	L	Y	G	U	R
K	Y	X	E	F	H	O	D	E
S	H	Z	G	I	K	I	B	A
A	E	U	H	A	D	L	G	S
D	A	I	L	Y	W	Y	J	Y
R	L	H	G	Q	Q	A	K	A
G	T	Q	I	W	B	P	L	Q
H	H	D	O	S	E	U	A	E
J	Y	J	P	M	O	E	B	Z
M	T	T	A	S	T	Y	N	U

RAFAEL GENTILE

2 Use the adjectives in exercise 1 to fill in the gaps. Use the glossary if necessary.

VAL THOERMER / SHUTTERSTOCK

Today I had lunch in a new restaurant near my house. I had thought it was a nice place, but I was wrong. The vegetables I ordered were very _____ and the soup was impossible to eat. It was too _____ so I had to drink lots of water. Then I decided to have a steak, but it was cold and _____. I was expecting some _____ and _____ food to improve my balanced _____ diet. But I didn't get any. I'll never go back to that restaurant again.

3 Read the tip and fill in the blanks with adverbs.

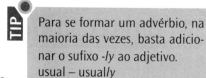

TIP

Para se formar um advérbio, na maioria das vezes, basta adicionar o sufixo -*ly* ao adjetivo.
usual – usual*ly*

a Her face was _____ (attractive) made up.

b The cable is _____ (strong) connected to the machine.

c These candies are _____ (artificial) flavored.

d There are some _____ (social) unacceptable behaviors in society.

e I'm a _____ (relative) lucky person.

f He talked _____ (sad) with her.

g Mary looks _____ (physical) stressed.

Appendix 1

page 164

4 Complete the table with a noun, an adjective, or an adverb.

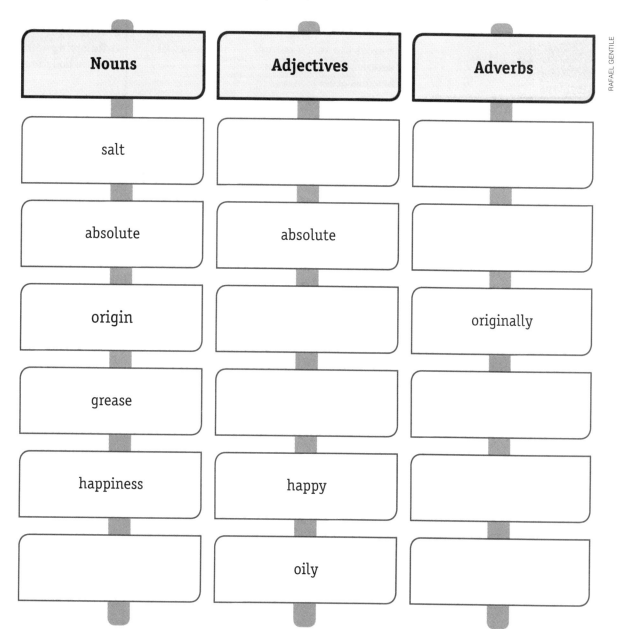

Nouns	Adjectives	Adverbs
salt		
absolute	absolute	
origin		originally
grease		
happiness	happy	
	oily	

Grammar in Use

REVIEW OF VERB TENSES

Tempo verbal	Formação	Uso	Expressões que comumente acompanham	Exemplos
Simple Present	• Infinitivo sem *to* + *-s/-es* para terceiras pessoas do singular. • Auxiliares: *do*, *does*, *don't* (*do + not*) e *doesn't* (*does + not*)	• ações rotineiras • fatos permanentes • ações futuras previamente agendadas • verdades universais • localizações geográficas	every day, always, sometimes, usually, never, on weekdays, etc.	Food nutrition labels **include** information on the serving size.
Present Continuous	• *To be* (presente) + verbo + *ing*	• ações em progresso no momento em que se fala • ações ocorrendo por um determinado período ou nos dias atuais • ações que foram agendadas, planejadas ou confirmadas anteriormente	now, right now, at the moment, nowadays, etc.	Nowadays, advertising **is influencing** young people's body image.
Going to (Future)	• *To be* (presente) + *going to* + verbo	• ações futuras com base em evidências do presente • intenções ou planos futuros • previsões	tomorrow, next..., in... days / weeks / years, tonight, etc.	Advertisers try to convince us that by buying their products we **are going to be** more attractive.
Imperative	• Afirmativa: infinitivo sem *to* • Negativa: *Don't* + infinitivo sem *to*	• ordens • pedidos • instruções	today, now, right now, at this moment, etc.	**Don't watch** the new movie. It's not as good as everybody says it is.
Simple Past	• Regulares: verbo + *-d/-ed* • Irregulares: formas específicas (ver lista na página 181) • Auxiliares: *did/ didn't* (*did + not*)	• ações que terminaram em um tempo determinado • hábitos no passado	last..., yesterday, ago, in..., etc.	**Did** the students **organize** an art exhibition last term?
Past Continuous	*To be* (passado) + verbo + *ing*	• ações em progresso em um determinado período no passado • uma ação que estava ocorrendo quando outra aconteceu • duas ou mais ações que ocorreram ao mesmo tempo no passado	when, while, yesterday, ago, last..., etc.	I **wasn't reading** the newspaper when you called.

1 Look at the cartoons. Circle the verbs and write the corresponding verb tenses.

"I'm retaining air."

"Do these plants make me look fat?"

"Then he had the nerve to say he likes plump women!"

"Honestly, Clara, that bikini leaves little to the imagination! And how long are you going to stand there, holding your stomachs in?"

DRIVE-THROUGH WEIGHT LOSS

"Try to get more exercise."

a _____

b _____

c _____

d _____

e _____

2 Use the words in the box to complete the sentences.

| now   today   tomorrow   yesterday   often   when |

a Are Matt and Jane going to play for the school team _____ morning?

b Sue _____ takes dance lessons on Saturdays.

c I wasn't surfing _____ I broke my finger. I was cooking!

d We met Janet's mom _____.

e Is Linda talking on the phone _____?

f Don't forget to bring my dictionary _____.

3 Choose the right alternative.

3.1 Jenny _____ a newspaper when her brother Tom _____ in.

   a ( ) reads; comes   **b** ( ) was reading; comes   **c** ( ) was reading; came

3.2 _____ your cell phones before the class begins.

   a ( ) Turn off   **b** ( ) Turns off   **c** ( ) Turned off

3.3 _____ the Thomsons _____ come for dinner tonight?

   a ( ) Are; coming   **b** ( ) Are; going   **c** ( ) Are; going to

3.4 I _____ everything I could to help Anna, but she failed the test anyway.

   a ( ) do   **b** ( ) did   **c** ( ) am doing

3.5 The teacher _____ the students to use the dictionary in tests.

   a ( ) doesn't allow   **b** ( ) allow   **c** ( ) going to allow

3.6 _____ Dennis and Silver _____ a lesson at this moment?

   a ( ) Do; attend   **b** ( ) Did; attend   **c** ( ) Are; attending

4 Read the magazine article and fill in the blanks using the verb forms in the box.

thought	are	do not participate	says
are beginning	showed	want	found

Girls and Body Image:
Loving the Skin She's in

"In America, we're obsessed with how we look," _____ Dr. Joan Lester, Director of Counseling and Psychological Services at Saint Joseph College. "Studies have found that by the 5th grade, girls _____ already _____ to diet, have already looked at themselves in the mirror and _____, 'I am fat.'" This is bad news for families because poor body image can lead to poor self-esteem, depression, and eating disorders. We all _____ our children to be healthy and to feel good about themselves – but in a society torn between an emaciated feminine ideal and skyrocketing rates of childhood obesity, how can parents help their daughters accept their bodies?

[…]

A 2006 study from the Girl Scout Research Institute titled *The New Normal? What Girls Say about Healthy Living* _____ that physically active girls are more satisfied with their weight and appearance than other girls, regardless of their weight. They're also more likely to lead a healthy lifestyle and less likely to be overweight. Sports _____ the key to feeling good; unfortunately, the same study _____ that 23% of girls _____ in sports because they feel that their bodies "do not look good."

[…]

Extracted from <http://www.education.com/magazine/article/Girls_and_Body_Image_Help_Your>.
Accessed on November 11, 2009.

Reading

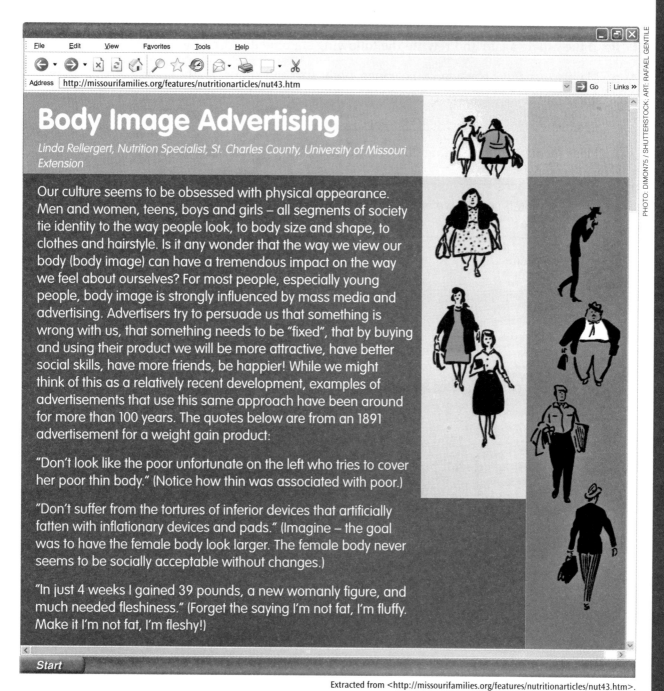

File   Edit   View   Favorites   Tools   Help

Address http://missourifamilies.org/features/nutritionarticles/nut43.htm   Go   Links »

Body Image Advertising

Linda Rellergert, Nutrition Specialist, St. Charles County, University of Missouri Extension

Our culture seems to be obsessed with physical appearance. Men and women, teens, boys and girls – all segments of society tie identity to the way people look, to body size and shape, to clothes and hairstyle. Is it any wonder that the way we view our body (body image) can have a tremendous impact on the way we feel about ourselves? For most people, especially young people, body image is strongly influenced by mass media and advertising. Advertisers try to persuade us that something is wrong with us, that something needs to be "fixed", that by buying and using their product we will be more attractive, have better social skills, have more friends, be happier! While we might think of this as a relatively recent development, examples of advertisements that use this same approach have been around for more than 100 years. The quotes below are from an 1891 advertisement for a weight gain product:

"Don't look like the poor unfortunate on the left who tries to cover her poor thin body." (Notice how thin was associated with poor.)

"Don't suffer from the tortures of inferior devices that artificially fatten with inflationary devices and pads." (Imagine – the goal was to have the female body look larger. The female body never seems to be socially acceptable without changes.)

"In just 4 weeks I gained 39 pounds, a new womanly figure, and much needed fleshiness." (Forget the saying I'm not fat, I'm fluffy. Make it I'm not fat, I'm fleshy!)

Start

Extracted from <http://missourifamilies.org/features/nutritionarticles/nut43.htm>.
Accessed on October 28, 2009.

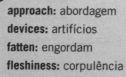

approach: abordagem	**pads:** enchimentos
devices: artifícios	**quotes:** citações
fatten: engordam	**tie identity to:** associam identidade com
fleshiness: corpulência	
fleshy: corpulento	**unfortunate:** infeliz
fluffy: fofo	**womanly:** própria da mulher

After Reading

1 Read the article again and rewrite the following statements correctly.

a Mainly teenagers consider appearance, body size and shape, clothes, and hairstyle to be important.

_____

b Mass media and advertising do not influence young people very much.

_____

c Advertisers tell us that we will be happier by having more friends and better social skills.

_____

d Advertisements that try to persuade clients are relatively recent.

_____

2 Read the following extracts.

"Our culture seems to be obsessed with physical **appearance**."

"While we might think of this as a relatively recent **development**, examples of **advertisements** that use this same approach have been around for more than 100 years."

"In just 4 weeks I gained 39 pounds, a new womanly figure, and much needed **fleshiness**."

In the extracts above, the words in bold are nouns formed by the suffixes -*ance*, -*ment*, and -*ness*. Take a look at the nouns below. Choose some of them to complete the sentences. Use the glossary if necessary.

agree – agreement	forgive – forgiveness
arrange – arrangement	guide – guidance
assist – assistance	happy – happiness
excite – excitement	sure – sureness

a The two countries finally reached an _____ and ended the war.

b There was great _____ among the children during the party.

c Susie found true _____ when she married Tony.

d I received financial _____ from my parents when I lost my job.

e _____ is all you need when you hurt somebody you love.

3 The number of people who read food nutrition labels has been increasing. More and more people want to have a balanced and healthy diet. Go back to pages 8 and 9. Take a look at the labels again. Then read the quotes below. Which product (the sour cream or chocolate pudding mix) is most appropriate for each person?

a "I usually buy cholesterol-free snacks for my kids." (Jane Watson, 30)

_____

b "It's important to have some carbs in my diet." (Bob Smith, 21)

_____

c "The doctor told me not to eat a lot of sodium." (Barbara Woods, 62)

_____

d "Snacks with fewer calories are always the best option." (Dr. Louis Stratford, 45)

_____

Language in Action

1 Timothy is an overweight American teenager. He has been trying to lose weight, but he can't. His mother is worried about his eating habits. They decide to attend a lecture on nutrition given by a well-known dietitian. They want to see if there is something else Timothy can do. Listen to part of the lecture and answer the questions.

a What is most teenagers' favorite kind of food?

_____

b What are two examples of junk food mentioned in the lecture?

_____

c Does a healthy diet include vegetables and grains?

_____

Reprodução proibida. Art.184 do Código Penal e Lei 9.610 de 19 de fevereiro de 1998.

BSIP / KEYSTOCK

2 Do you and your classmates have similar eating habits? Answer the questionnaire. Then interview two classmates. Take notes.

	You	Classmate 1	Classmate 2
What do you usually have for breakfast?			
How often do you eat pasta?			
What are your favorite vegetables?			
Do you like fruits? Which ones?			
What kind of meat do you prefer?			
Do you eat much oily food?			

Picture Dictionary 1
page 156

3 Now present the results of your survey to your classmates. Use the expressions in bold. Some examples are given.

> **One of us** eats pasta twice a week.
>
> **Two of us** prefer fish to red meat.
>
> **All of us** have yogurt for breakfast.
>
> **None of us** like vegetables.

Writing

Timothy lives in Ohio, but he has a few e-pals in other states nearby. Nick is one of them. In fact, he is Timothy's best friend. He lives in New York. Read the last e-mail Nick sent to Timothy.

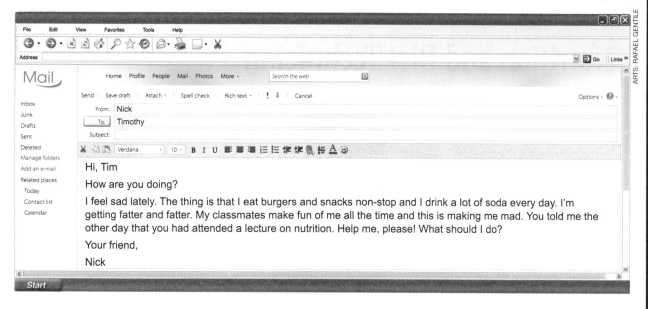

If you were Tim, what advice would you give Nick? Use some of the expressions below to write him an e-mail.

cycle or walk to school	exercise	fish	healthy diet	juice or water	junk food
listen to what your classmates say		red meat	snacks and desserts		vegetables and fruit

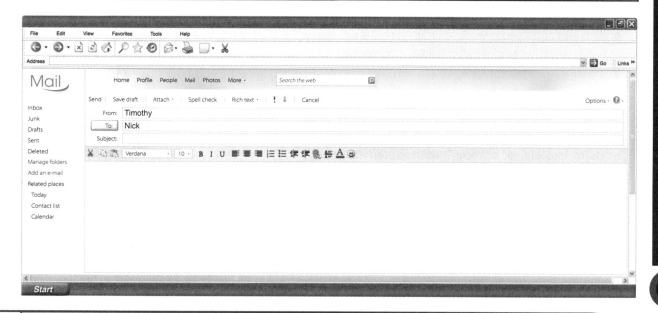

Consultando outras fontes

filmes: *Delírio de consumo de Becky Bloom* (EUA, 2009; direção: P. J. Hogan)
O diabo veste Prada (EUA, 2006; direção: David Frankel)

livro: *Mentes insaciáveis: anorexia, bulimia e compulsão alimentar* (Ediouro; autora: Ana Beatriz Barbosa Silva)

música: "Fashion" (Lady Gaga)

Nutrition and Diet Technician

Nowadays, it's very common to say that "you are what you eat." Well, in this case, a nutrition and diet technician would come in handy! After all, this person's job consists mainly of assisting with quality control and coordinating the execution of meals – from the size of the portions to transport and distribution.

This professional takes people's measurements to determine their ideal diet, as well as to elaborate balanced menus according to specific rules that promote a healthy lifestyle – when it comes to food, at least. This work is based on biological studies, since a nutrition and diet technician has to understand how a human body works and how it's *supposed* to work, in order to bring the former as close as possible to the latter.

Basically, a nutrition and diet technician can work anywhere food is sold or served. This includes all kinds of restaurants, schools, health

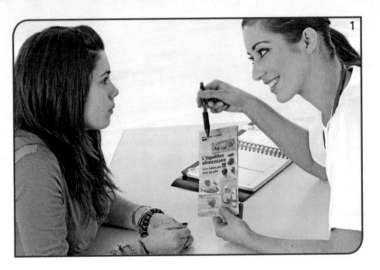

clinics, military institutions, among many other places. A nutrition and diet technician can also work in any food production site, but no matter where this professional works, he or she will always be supervised by a nutritionist.

In order to become such a professional, a person has to take a course for twelve hundred hours, which includes an eighty-hour apprenticeship.

Based on <http://www.bls.gov/oco/ocos077.htm>; <http://www.nutritionsociety.org>;
<http://education-portal.com/directory/category/Medical_and_Health_Professions/Nutrition_Services/Djetetic_Technician_-_DTR.html>;
<http://www.careerplanner.com/DOT-Job-Descriptions/DIETETIC-TECHNICIAN.cfm>.
Accessed on January 21, 2010.

at least: pelo menos

in order to bring the former as close as possible to the latter: de forma que o primeiro (como o corpo humano funciona) se aproxime o máximo possível do segundo (como o corpo humano deveria funcionar)

measurements: medidas

production site: local de produção

twelve hundred: one thousand and two hundred = 1200

when it comes to: quando se trata de, quando o assunto é

would come in handy: seria útil

Para mais informações, acesse:

<http://catalogonct.mec.gov.br/et_ambiente_saude_seguranca/t_nutricao_dietetica.php>;

<http://www.sp.senac.br/jsp/default.jsp?newsID=DYNAMIC,oracle.br.dataservers.CourseDataServer,selectCourse&course=164&template=380.dwt&unit=NONE&testeira=474>;

<http://www.centropaulasouza.sp.gov.br/Cursos/ETE/nutricao-dietetica.html>.

1 Você gostaria de ser técnico em nutrição e dietética? Por quê? / Por que não?

2 Match the photos with their corresponding words.

SCIENCEPHOTOS / ALAMY / OTHER IMAGES

A

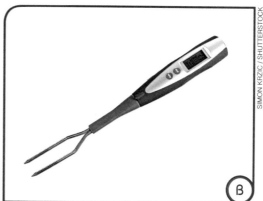

SIMON KRZIC / SHUTTERSTOCK

B

TOKIO MAPLE / SHUTTERSTOCK

C

MTR / SHUTTERSTOCK

D

AFANASYEV DENIS / SHUTTERSTOCK

E

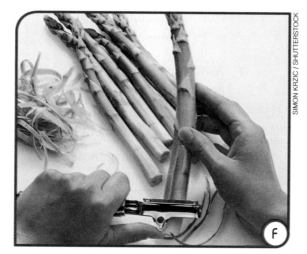

SIMON KRZIC / SHUTTERSTOCK

F

(   ) vegetable peeler

(   ) electronic scale

(   ) blender

(   ) test tube

(   ) ladle

(   ) thermometer

Additional Practice

For exercises 1 to 10, choose the best alternative.

1 "Variations in the physical _____ of humans, known as human looks, are believed by anthropologists to be an important factor in the development of personality and social relations, in particular, physical attractiveness. [...]"

Extracted from <http://en.wikipedia.org/wiki/Human_physical_appearance>.
Accessed on January 29, 2010.

a ( ) assistance
b ( ) appearance
c ( ) guidance
d ( ) excitement
e ( ) agreement

2 Being _____ active for 30 to 60 minutes at least four times a week can help you to build strength and fitness, to relax and reduce stress, to gain more energy, and to improve your sleep.

Based on <http://www.healthierus.gov/exercise.html>.
Accessed on January 29, 2010.

a ( ) physical
b ( ) daily
c ( ) easily
d ( ) physic
e ( ) physically

3 Studies show that the vitamins in the food are _____ the vitamins in the supplements, and are _____ because of the other components of the food.

Adapted from <http://www.explorevitamins.co.uk/are-vitamins-food-better-than-supplements.html>.
Accessed on January 29, 2010.

a ( ) good than, effective
b ( ) better than, more effective
c ( ) best than, more effective
d ( ) better than, most effective
e ( ) best than, more effective

4 Christie is helping her mom with a menu for their Saturday night guests. They can't decide what to serve because _____ is a vegetarian. On the other hand, _____ love cheese.

a ( ) all of them, one of them
b ( ) one of them, all of them
c ( ) one of them, one of them
d ( ) two of them, none of them
e ( ) all of them, none of them

5 A: We have a Spanish test and I can't memorize all the vocabulary.

B: _____! The teacher _____ us to use a dictionary.

a ( ) Don't worry, allows
b ( ) Doesn't worry, allow
c ( ) Worried, allowed
d ( ) Worry, allowing
e ( ) Don't worry, is allow

6 The teens _____ the instructions easy to follow and soon all of them _____ along well.

a ( ) found, were getting
b ( ) found, is getting
c ( ) found, are getting
d ( ) found, was getting
e ( ) found, got

7 A: Your cell phone _____. Why don't you answer it?

B: I can't talk right now. I _____ this project and I have to finish it before class.

a ( ) am ringing; is doing
b ( ) is ringing; am doing
c ( ) rings; does
d ( ) ring; do
e ( ) is ring; is do

8 **Ashley:** I've been looking for Zach all morning. Do you know where he is?

Madison: He _____ for the school team tomorrow. So today they _____ all morning and afternoon.

a (   ) goes to play, are practicing

b (   ) plays, practices

c (   ) play, practice

d (   ) is going to play, are practicing

e (   ) playing, practicing

9 **Veronica:** What happened to Rachel? She _____ so different. Is she sick?

Jordan: You know, girls are so concerned about their looks. A while ago she _____ to go on a diet and she went too far. Now she's being assisted by a nutritionist.

a (   ) is looking; decides

b (   ) looked; decides

c (   ) look; decide

d (   ) looks; is deciding

e (   ) looks; decided

10 **Mathew:** Did you watch the game yesterday? It was terrific!

Joshua: I couldn't. I _____.

a (   ) is doing my homework

b (   ) are doing my homework

c (   ) was doing my homework

d (   ) were doing my homework

e (   ) is going to do my homework

Refletindo sobre sua aprendizagem

Ao final desta unidade, você já é capaz de:

- Compreender rótulos; identificar e comparar informações nutricionais. ☐
- Reconhecer alguns adjetivos e advérbios formados pelo acréscimo dos sufixos -y e -ly e utilizá-los em diferentes contextos. ☐
- Reconhecer alguns substantivos formados pelos sufixos -ance, -ment e -ness e utilizá-los em diferentes contextos. ☐
- Utilizar diferentes tempos verbais em variadas situações comunicativas. ☐
- Coletar informações e reproduzi-las. ☐
- Expressar-se adequadamente para dar um conselho. ☐

Aprimorando sua aprendizagem

- Peça ajuda ao professor ou aos colegas para que esclareçam suas dúvidas.
- Refaça os exercícios.
- Visite a biblioteca da sua escola ou uma biblioteca pública e consulte livros de gramática e/ou faça leituras de seu interesse.
- Assista a filmes em inglês.

PRE-READING

Look at the map. In your opinion, what does the green part represent?

Amazon Biome

The biome occupies an area of 4,196,943 km², which represents more than 40% of the country and consists mostly of tropical forest. The Amazon is in the states of Acre, Amapá, Amazonas, Pará, and Roraima, and certain regions of Maranhão, Mato Grosso, Rondônia, and Tocantins states. The Amazon is made up of different ecosystems and dense forests, deciduous forests, flooded fields, meadows, grasslands, mountain refuges, and pioneer formations.

Even though this biome is the most preserved, about 16% of its area has been destroyed, which is equivalent to two times the area of São Paulo state.

Deforestation, fires, mining, biopiracy, and agro-pasture represent the main environmental problems in the Amazon biome. All these actions are responsible for severe climate changes on the planet – like global warming.

The Amazon is considered a great atmosphere "cooler" and it is the world's largest biodiversity shelter. Some research indicates that in the Amazon there are about thirty million species of animals.

Extracted from <http://www.ibflorestas.org.br/en/amazon-biome.html>.
Accessed on February 1, 2010.

"Gentilmente cedido por Cristina Leite, autora e tradutora do texto."

biome: bioma

deciduous forests: florestas decíduas (florestas da zona temperada que perdem suas folhas durante o outono para suportar o frio do inverno)

grasslands: pastos

meadows: prados (campos cobertos de plantas herbáceas que servem para pastagem)

After Reading

1 Write T (true) or F (false). Correct the false sentences.

a ( ) All the states in the North, Northeast, and Central-West regions of Brazil are part of the Amazon biome.

_____

_____

b ( ) The Amazon biome is the most-preserved biome in Brazil.

_____

_____

c ( ) The area destroyed in the Amazon biome corresponds to the area of the state of São Paulo.

_____

_____

d ( ) Natural disasters represent the main problems in the Amazon biome.

_____

_____

2 Choose the best synonym for the words in bold.

2.1 "The Amazon is **made up** of different ecosystems […]"

    a ( ) done

    b ( ) composed

    c ( ) put in order

2.2 "The Amazon is considered a great atmosphere "cooler" and it is the world's largest biodiversity **shelter**."

    a ( ) an area of protection and safety

    b ( ) a place to live or stay, considered as a basic human need

    c ( ) a place for people without a home

3 According to the text, what do the numbers below represent? Write your answer in Portuguese.

a 4,196,943   _____

b 40%   _____

c 16%   _____

d 30,000,000   _____

4 Leia o extrato de texto abaixo e discuta-o com seus colegas.

> "O termo biopirataria foi lançado em 1993 pela ONG RAFI (hoje ETC-Group) para alertar sobre o fato de que recursos biológicos e conhecimento indígena estavam sendo apanhados e patenteados por empresas multinacionais e instituições científicas e que as comunidades que durante séculos usam esses recursos e geraram esses conhecimentos não estão participando dos lucros."

Extraído de <http://www.amazonlink.org/biopirataria/biopirataria_faq.htm>.
Acessado em 23 de novembro de 2009.

a Em sua opinião, as empresas multinacionais e as instituições científicas têm o direito de se apropriar desses recursos e do conhecimento? Por quê?

b Baseado na afirmação acima, você acha que os recursos naturais da Amazônia vão esgotar-se em alguns anos?

Vocabulary in Use

1 Read the following entry from a dictionary and do the activity.

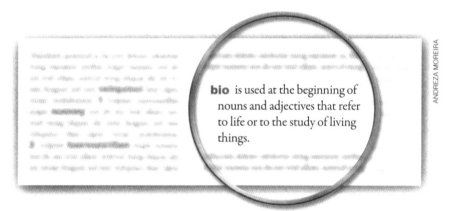

bio is used at the beginning of nouns and adjectives that refer to life or to the study of living things.

COLLINS *Cobuild English Dictionary for Advanced Learners*. 3. ed. London: Harper-Collins, 2001.

Use the words in the box to label the other entries below.

> biodegradable   biodiversity   bioengineering   biology   biotechnology

a the scientific study of the life and structure of plants and animals _____

b the use of living cells and bacteria in industrial and scientific processes

_____

c the use of engineering methods to solve medical problems – for example, the use of artificial arms and legs _____

d the existence of a large number of different kinds of animals and plants which make a balanced environment _____

e something that can be changed to a harmless natural state by the action of bacteria, and will therefore not damage the environment _____

Appendix 2

page 165

Extracted from *Oxford Advanced Learner's Dictionary*. 7. ed. São Paulo: Oxford do Brasil, 2005. p. 141-142.

ANDREZA MOREIRA

2 Fill in the chart based on the information in the tip. Then translate the new words. Letter *a* is done for you.

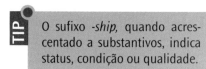

a	owner	*ownership*	*propriedade*
b	friend		
c	relation		
d	member		
e	champion		
f	leader		

3 Complete the sentences with words from exercise 2.

a I have decided to sign up for a _____ to Greenpeace.

b Holland won the European _____ some time ago.

c She has a close _____ with her daughter.

d Professor Ross has great faith in his own _____ abilities.

e The _____ between Adriana and her new neighbor is growing stronger.

f Claiming _____ of genetic resources and traditional knowledge is considered as biopiracy.

Grammar in Use

SIMPLE FUTURE

FORMAÇÃO: **WILL** + VERBO NO INFINITIVO SEM A PARTÍCULA **TO**	
Forma afirmativa	In coming years, biopiracy **will cause** traditional populations to lose control over their resources.
Forma negativa	Flora and fauna **won't (will + not) disappear** from Brazil in the next few years.
Forma interrogativa	**A: Will** the Amazon rainforest **recover** from deforestation? **B:** Yes, it will. / No, it won't.

USO	
O **Simple Future** é utilizado para:	
• Expressar ação ou previsão quanto ao futuro.	We **will** never **forget** about our teacher Ms. Miller.
• Fazer um pedido.	**Will** you please **bring** me your umbrella?
Geralmente vem acompanhado de advérbios ou expressões como **tomorrow**, **next**..., **in**..., **on**..., etc.	

27

1 Use the Simple Future to complete the sentences.

a _____ Doris _____ (come) home early today?

b Their plane _____ (land) in 2 hours.

c We _____ (visit – neg.) grandma until she leaves the hospital.

d _____ you _____ (answer) the phone for me?

e I _____ (express – neg.) my feelings to a man I hardly know.

2 Look at the pictures. Then complete the sentences using *will/won't* + the verbs in the box.

have   play   rain   study

a It _____
later.

b He _____
tomorrow.

c I _____
fish for dinner.

d They _____
the drums in the show.

3 Use the cues to write questions with *will*. Then write short answers.

a it / rain / today / (yes)

A: Will it rain today?

B: Yes, it will.

b the chef / suggest / the main course of our dinner / (no)

A: _____

B: _____

c you / accept / the job offer / (no)

A: _____

B: _____

d the girl / ask her brother to go with her / tonight / (yes)

A: _____

B: _____

e they / enjoy / the match / next weekend / (yes)

A: _____

B: _____

f the company / launch a new product / soon / (no)

A: _____

B: _____

4 Express your opinion about the issues below. Use the cues to write sentences with *will/won't* and *probably* or *definitely*. Letter *a* is done for you.

a robots / perform / household chores

Robots will definitely/probably perform household chores.

Robots probably won't perform household chores.

Robots definitely won't perform household chores.

b cars / fly / in ten years

_____

_____

c people from different cities / carpool

_____

_____

d tennis / be the most popular sport in Brazil / in the future

_____

_____

e fauna and flora / continue to disappear in the Amazon / during the coming years

_____

_____

5 Based on the information given, complete the sentences with *will/won't*. Use the verbs in parentheses. Look at the example.

a Scientists are developing new medicines to cure some diseases. (cure)
New medicines *will cure some diseases*.

b More and more, we are suffering from the effects of global warming. (affect)
Global warming _____.

c Poor young girls are getting jobs for financial support. (support)
Getting jobs _____.

d Globalization isn't harmful for the growth of the population. (harm)
Globalization _____.

e The hacker is creating a virus to gain access to banking accounts. (gain access)
Using a virus, _____.

FUTURE CONTINUOUS

FORMAÇÃO: **WILL BE** + VERBO + **ING**

Forma afirmativa	Class 101 **will be going** on a field trip at 7 o'clock tomorrow.
Forma negativa	The Gordons **won't be traveling** abroad on their next vacation.
Forma interrogativa	**A: Will** you **be working** tomorrow morning? **B:** Yes, I/we will. / No, I/we won't.

USO

O **Future Continuous** é utilizado para:	
• Expressar uma ação que estará ocorrendo em um determinado tempo no futuro.	Third-world communities are sure they **will be paying** a high price for biopiracy in the future.

6 Change the sentences into the negative and interrogative forms. Then answer the questions according to the cues in parentheses.

a You will be teaching a new group next semester. (no)

_____

_____

_____

b We will call him when we finish our assignment. (yes)

_____

_____

_____

c The new environmental law will have a strong impact on us. (yes)

_____

_____

_____

d The young boys will be playing soccer at school at nine tomorrow. (no)

_____

_____

_____

e Jonathan will come later tonight. (yes)

_____

_____

_____

7 Match the sentences.

a I will send…

b Rose will call it a day…

c They will certainly invite us…

d Our team will be playing…

e The cleaning ladies will be sweeping…

( ) because she is tired and sleepy.

( ) against yours tomorrow evening.

( ) the e-mails as soon as I finish typing them.

( ) the floor in an hour.

( ) to their birthday party.

Reading

BIOPIRACY IN THE AMAZON – HISTORICAL FACTS

FABIO COLOMBINI

Pau-brasil

Biopiracy in the Amazon began almost immediately after the "discovery" of the region by the Portuguese in 1500, when they stole the secret – from the indigenous people of the region – of how to extract a red pigment from *pau-brasil* (brazil wood). Emblematic of today's situation, in which flora and fauna continue to disappear, the wood that gave Brazil its name has completely disappeared and is now preserved only in a few botanical gardens.

WOLFGANG KAEHLER / CORBIS / CORBIS (DC) / LATINSTOCK

Rubber

An infamous case of biopiracy is that of Englishman Henry Alexander Wickham, who in 1876 took rubber tree seeds – some say he hid them between banana leaves – to a new plantation of *Hevea brasiliensis* in the British colonies in Malaysia. In a few decades the region would become the main exporter of latex, ruining the rubber-tree based Amazon economy. Wickham was knighted by King George V and loathed by Brazil's rubber barons, who called him "the executioner of Amazonas".

KJELL B. SANDVED / PHOTORESEARCHERS / LATINSTOCK

Quinine

Another example of biopiracy is the malaria drug quinine. The indigenous people used the plant as an infusion in fever treatment. Derived from the cinchona tree (*Cinchona officinalis*), it was used in the '20s in the U.S. for the treatment of malaria. Known as Indian fever bark, the product was used in Europe since the early 1500s. (One century later its name was changed to Jesuit fever bark.) The demand for cinchona almost made it extinct. By smuggling it from South America to Java, in 1865, Englishman Charles Ledger saved the plant. And – sixty years later – more than 95% of the world's quinine was coming from Java.

[…]

Start

Extracted from <http://www.amazonlink.org/biopiracy/biopiracy_history.htm>.
Accessed on October 28, 2009.

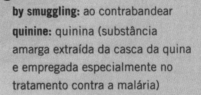

by smuggling: ao contrabandear
quinine: quinina (substância amarga extraída da casca da quina e empregada especialmente no tratamento contra a malária)
ruining: destruindo
seeds: sementes
wood: madeira

After Reading

1 Answer the questions below in Portuguese.

a When did biopiracy begin in the Amazon?

_____

_____

_____

b What did Henry Alexander Wickham do in 1876?

_____

_____

_____

c How did Charles Ledger contribute to save quinine?

_____

_____

_____

2 In which paragraphs can you find the following information?

a (   ) Malaysia became the main exporter of latex.

b (   ) The wood that gave Brazil its name has completely disappeared.

c (   ) A plant was used as medicine in the '20s.

3 According to the text we can infer that:

a (   ) Brazil profits greatly from biopiracy.

b (   ) The Brazilian people are victims of biopiracy.

c (   ) Only indigenous people know about medicinal plants.

4 Both texts in this unit present factual descriptions. Read the texts again and mark their main characteristics below.

a (   ) They have a comic tone.

b (   ) They are published only in specialized magazines.

c (   ) They are based on real facts.

d (   ) They express personal opinions.

e (   ) They have previously gathered information.

f (   ) They present charts, numbers, dates, etc.

Language in Action

1 Jorge is a Brazilian young man. He has just finished a technical course in tourism and is now
working part-time as a tour guide at a hotel in the Amazon. Today he is attending a lecture
about the Boi-Bumbá festival. Listen to part of the lecture and fill in the blanks. Use the words
in the box.

> boat   floats   Indians   lifetime   story

The Boi-Bumbá festival brings the city of Parintins to life. 35,000 people arrive

by _____ and 2,000 by plane to join the two colorful troupes of

characters (O Garantido and O Caprichoso) that tell the _____ of

Amazon folklore. This atmospheric festival takes place in the Bumbódromo and there

you can see a fantastic folklore spectacle created by _____ in the

middle of the jungle. It is a once-in-a-_____ privilege to assist this

opera of the jungle with its costumes, beautifully dressed flag bearers, and decorated

_____ – all moving to the different Indian rhythms.

[...]

Extracted from <http://www.themanual2brazil.com/Destination/Manaus/Package/Parintins-Festival-by-Plane.aspx>.
Accessed on February 5, 2010.

2 Two weeks after that lecture, some British tourists arrived at the hotel. Jorge had to give them
some suggestions on what to do in the area. Read the dialogue between Jorge and a tourist.
In pairs, make new dialogues. Use the Picture Dictionary 2 on page 157. You can use some
expressions in the boxes, too.

Tourist: What should we do today?
Jorge: What about sport fishing?
Tourist: I'd love to do that.

Jorge
What about...?
Why don't you...?
Would you like to...?

Tourist
I'd love to do that.
That's a great idea!
That sounds perfect.
I don't think that's a good idea.

34

Picture Dictionary 2
page 157

Writing

Think of some interesting things a visitor can do in your city. Create a flyer. Paste photos or do drawings to illustrate the flyer. Write captions under the photos/pictures. Exchange books with other classmates and compare your flyers.

RAFAEL GENTILE

Consultando outras fontes

documentários: *Aldeias vigilantes* (Animação de 9 minutos disponível em: <http://www.youtube.com/watch?v=tQf2aGBZZCY>. Acessado em 6 de fevereiro de 2010.)
O sabor do cupuaçu (Disponível em: <http://www2.tvcultura.com.br/reportereco/materia.asp?materiaid=68>. Acessado em 6 de fevereiro de 2010.)

livro: *Biopirataria: pilhagem da natureza e do conhecimento* (Vozes; autor: Vandana Shiva)

Lawyer

Do you want to combat environmental crimes, as well as any other kind of felony or transgression, and make things right? Then you can become a lawyer.

Lawyers (also known as attorneys) work to make everybody – people, companies, and the government – abide by laws, rules, and regulations. In order to do this, lawyers study laws and use these laws to prevent their clients from being harmed in any way – physically, morally, or financially.

These professionals write legal documents, represent their clients in criminal and civil trials, advise them about their legal rights and obligations, and lead civil and criminal lawsuits. They also settle labor disputes, instruct corporate clients during business transactions, litigate divorces, prepare wills and business contracts, among many other responsibilities.

There are many law fields to choose from when you become a lawyer, including environmental, international, criminal, labor, family, intellectual property, and information technology.

Lawyers can work in corporations, law firms, insurance companies, banks, non-profit organizations, or they can be self-employed and have their own offices. They can also work for the government as judges, public defenders, prosecutors, magistrates, and so on.

Law school is five-years long and apprenticeship is mandatory. After graduating from college, you must pass the written examination of the Brazilian Bar Association (OAB), otherwise you won't be allowed to legally practice law.

Based on <http://www.jobprofiles.org/programs/legal.htm>; <http://www.wisegeek.com/what-does-an-attorney-do.htm>; <http://education-portal.com/search/quicksearch.html>. Accessed on February 6, 2010.

abide by: obedecer
felony: crime muito sério
harmed: prejudicado(a)
intellectual property: propriedade intelectual
judges: juízes
labor: trabalhistas

lawsuits: ações judiciais, processos
lead: conduzem
litigate: pleiteam em juízo
magistrates: magistrados
mandatory: obrigatório de acordo com a lei, exigido por lei

non-profit organizations: organizações sem fins lucrativos
otherwise: caso contrário
prosecutors: promotores
settle: resolvem
trials: julgamentos, processos
wills: testamentos

Para mais informações, acesse:

<http://guiadoestudante.abril.com.br/profissoes/ciencias-humanas-sociais/profissoes_271600.shtml>;

<http://www.brasilprofissoes.com.br/verprof.php?codigo=4>;

<http://www.suapesquisa.com/cursos/curso_direito.htm>;

<http://www.oab.org.br>.

1 Você gostaria de ser advogado(a)? Por quê? / Por que não?

2 Look at the photo below. Then fill in the gaps with the appropriate words.

courtroom

judge

lawyer

jury

witness

accused

a Everybody in the _____ remained in complete silence to hear the _____ announce the verdict.

b If the _____ was hiding under his bed when the house was robbed, how could he have seen the crime?

c The company hired the best _____ in the city to write the legal documents.

d The _____ retired to consider their verdict.

e The _____ was found innocent.

Additional Practice

For exercises 1 to 9, choose the best alternative.

1 On Valentine's Day in the USA people give each other poems to strenghten their bond of _____.

a ( ) membership
b ( ) friendship
c ( ) championship
d ( ) leadership
e ( ) ownership

2 "[...] The Amazon River basin rainforest contains a wider variety of plant and animal life than any other _____ in the world. [...]"

Extracted from <www.blueplanetbiomes.org/rainforest.htm>. Accessed on February 6, 2010.

a ( ) river
b ( ) meadow
c ( ) biome
d ( ) grassland
e ( ) biology

3 "Representatives from patent offices in six Latin American nations that share the Amazon basin have agreed to work together against _____ – the unauthorized commercial exploitation of their native species.

According to the Rio Declaration – signed in Rio de Janeiro, Brazil, on July 1 – Bolivia, Brazil, Ecuador, Peru, Surinam, and Venezuela will share information and jointly develop policies to tackle the phenomenon. [...]"

Extracted from <http://www.scidev.net/en/agriculture-and-environment/news/amazon-countries-team-up-to-tackle-biopiracy.html> Accessed on February 6, 2010.

a ( ) biodegradable
b ( ) biology
c ( ) biodiversity
d ( ) biopiracy
e ( ) biological

4 George: Hi, Hanna. How's it going?
Hanna: Good. How about you?
George: Not that good. I have to travel next weekend and can't take my dog with me.
Hanna: Don't worry. I _____ of Sam for you.
George: Thanks, you're a life saver!

a ( ) will take care
b ( ) going to take care
c ( ) will go take care
d ( ) am going to care
e ( ) is going to care

5 Some studies claim that physical exercise _____ you thin. They say that exercise makes you hungry and that we often reward ourselves afterward by eating the junk food we like.

a ( ) is going to
b ( ) will go
c ( ) are going to
d ( ) won't make
e ( ) aren't going

6 A: This is such a perfect Saturday – sunny and hot. What should we do?
B: Would you like to go swimming?
A: _____

a ( ) What about you?
b ( ) Won't you?
c ( ) Will you?
d ( ) I'm not.
e ( ) I'd love to.

7 A: He _____ at the library tonight in case anything happens and you need to contact him, OK?
B: No problem.

a ( ) will studying
b ( ) will be studying
c ( ) will go
d ( ) goes
e ( ) is going

8 A: Can I call you later?

B: Well, I've got lots of things to do.

A: Oh, really? What _____ at nine?

a ( ) will you be doing

b ( ) will be doing

c ( ) will doing

d ( ) you be doing

e ( ) be you doing

9 It's raining cats and dogs. _____ me my umbrella, please?

a ( ) You bring

b ( ) Bring you will

c ( ) Will you bring

d ( ) You will bring

e ( ) Bring will you

10 Complete part of the lyrics of "Promise", by Akon:

[…]

I promise U, I _____ there for U.

Whether sun or rain or season change.

[…]

a ( ) am going be

b ( ) going to be

c ( ) 'll going to be

d ( ) 'll go

e ( ) 'll be

Refletindo sobre sua aprendizagem

Ao final desta unidade, você já é capaz de:

• Ler um mapa, refletir sobre ele e confrontar as opiniões com as informações contidas na parte verbal do texto. ☐

• Localizar informações específicas no texto, analisá-las e corrigi-las, se necessário. ☐

• Identificar sinônimos para algumas palavras/expressões relacionadas ao tema do texto. ☐

• Interpretar dados numéricos de acordo com o contexto em que se encontram. ☐

• Expressar pontos de vista em relação ao problema da biopirataria e discutir possíveis soluções com os colegas da sala e com o professor. ☐

• Relacionar novas palavras às suas definições. ☐

• Produzir novos substantivos, formados pelo acréscimo do sufixo -ship e usá-los em contextos diversos. ☐

• Reconhecer o emprego e a função comunicativa de verbos no *Simple Future* e no *Future Continuous*. ☐

• Produzir frases afirmativas e negativas com *definitely* e *probably* para expressar opiniões sobre assuntos diversos. ☐

• Usar a língua portuguesa como mediadora na compreensão de um texto. ☐

• Fazer inferências como uma estratégia de leitura. ☐

• Reconhecer as principais características de textos descritivos relacionados a fatos. ☐

• Usar a linguagem oral para fazer sugestões e expressar opiniões sobre sugestões feitas a você. ☐

• Produzir um folheto turístico. ☐

Aprimorando sua aprendizagem

• Peça ajuda ao professor ou aos colegas para que esclareçam suas dúvidas.

• Refaça os exercícios.

• Visite a biblioteca da sua escola ou uma biblioteca pública e consulte livros de gramática e/ou faça leituras de seu interesse.

• Assista a filmes em inglês.

1 Classify the words in bold according to their context. Write them down in the corresponding diagram.

a Slow down, please. You're driving so **fast**!

b The view from that point is just **incredible**. Go up and see it.

c You must make some **hard** decisions this year, honey.

d **Luckily** the museum was still open at that time.

e **Ironically**, he felt much better when he was fired.

f Life is never **dull** when they are at home.

g Students should read the text and decide if the statements are **true** or false.

h She can't work **well** under pressure.

i He married in his **late** twenties.

j We didn't go **far**.

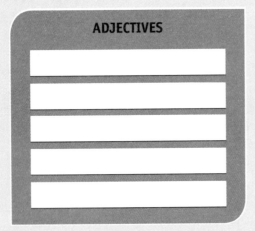

ADJECTIVES

ADVERBS

2 Complete the sentences with the correct form of the verbs given.

a agree – expect (neg.) – go – read (2x)

Every time Theo _____ to bed, he _____ a different book. The

one he _____ now is *Iracema*, by José de Alencar. His Portuguese teacher said,

"_____ *Iracema* to be a funny novel." He _____ with his teacher.

Iracema is extremely sad.

b be – enjoy – stay – travel

Last summer her family _____ to a city near theirs. They _____ at a fancy hotel in front of the beach. It _____ fantastic. This year they _____ the beaches in Miami.

c be (2x) – get – have – know (neg.)

I _____ lunch with my friend Jamil when my mother _____ home. She _____ very upset. I still _____ why. She _____ always happy and lively.

3 Rewrite the sentences using the words in parentheses. Make all the necessary changes.

    a Adrian wakes up at seven every day. (yesterday)

    _____
    _____

    b Ursula played a video game all morning. Her mother called her. (when)

    _____
    _____

    c Ross watched fantastic black-and-white movies on the weekend. (often)

    _____
    _____

    d The teacher ordered students not to use cell phones in class. (Don't)

    _____
    _____

    e Toby and Pauline are traveling to the Caribbean in July. (going to)

    _____
    _____

4 The following text presents some predictions about Jupiter in the year 2087. Fill in the gaps with *will* or *won't*. Use the verbs in parentheses.

Do you really think there _____ (be) life on Jupiter in 2087? I don't know, but I think it's quite difficult. It's so distant from Earth that it _____ (cost) a lot of money to reach that planet. There is no air. So people _____ (live) in huge domes. Human beings _____ (be) able to leave them because the temperature outside is freezing cold. However, I do believe Earth _____ (be) overcrowded in the year 2087 and maybe we _____ (have) good living conditions here.

5 Underline the appropriate alternative.

a **A:** What do you expect to be doing this time next year?

   B: I know what **I'll be doing / will do**. **I'll be taking / I'll take** a computer course.

b It's very hot in here. **I'll be opening / I'll open** the window.

c I can't meet you at 10. **I'll be having / I'll have** yoga classes.

d In the year 2051, cars **will be flying / will fly**.

e In twenty years' time, robots **will be doing / will do** all sorts of household chores.

f Good luck with the exam. **I'll think / 'll be thinking** of you.

g Where **will you all spend / will you all be spending** the night?

6 Jenny and Mia are making plans for the following Friday. Complete their dialogue. Use the information in the box and the Future Continuous.

> 10 a.m. – work on the Biology project
>
> 12:30 p.m. – lunch with Sarah
>
> 1:45 p.m. – do homework
>
> 5 p.m. – play volleyball at the club

Jenny: Hey, what's up? Shall we meet at about 10?

Mia: I'm afraid I can't. I _____ at 10.

Jenny: How about lunch, then?

Mia: I'm sorry, but _____.

Jenny: Really? So why don't we meet after lunch?

Mia: Well... I _____ and I really don't

know how long it will take.

Jenny: Can I go to your place around 5?

Mia: Not really. I _____.

Jenny: What about some pizza at 8?

Mia: It sounds perfect to me.

7 The media's influence on teenagers and their eating habits might lead to something very serious: an eating disorder. Read the text and write T (true) or F (false). Correct the false statements.

Eating Disorders: *By the Numbers*

RAFAEL GENTILE

According to NIMH and ANAD statistics:

0.5-3.7% of Americans have anorexia.

1.1-4.2% of Americans have bulimia.

Up to **50%** of patients with anorexia develop bulimic symptoms.

10% of anorexics are male.

20-30% of younger anorexics are male.

Mortality rates for anorexia increase by roughly **0.5%** per year.

Mortality rates for anorexia are upward of **20%** in patients who have had the illness for more than 20 years.

Extracted from <http://www.psychweekly.com/aspx/article/ArticleDetail.aspx?articleid=124>. Accessed on February 8, 2010.

a (   ) Over 4% of the American population has anorexia.

_____

b (   ) Bulimia is more present in Americans' lives than anorexia.

_____

c (   ) We can infer that anorexia often leads to bulimia.

_____

d (   ) 85% of anorexics are female.

_____

e (   ) Mortality rates for anorexia increase by exactly 0.5% per year.

_____

f (   ) Mortality rates are higher in patients who have had anorexia for over two decades.

_____

3 Being a Volunteer

PRE-READING

What is the poster about? Is it possible to know when this poster was published?

Corporate Volunteering Survey in Brazil

CBVE

2009

Conselho Brasileiro de Voluntariado Empresarial

**Brazil needs to know.
Your company should participate.
You should respond to this survey.**

Having more information about corporate volunteering in Brazil is fundamental in order to motivate changes and new challenges to the sector.

Large, medium, small and micro-businesses should take part in this survey. By doing so, they will help to write the story of volunteering in this country.

Respond to the survey at www.riovoluntario.org.br and take part in one of the largest studies ever performed on Brazilian Corporate Volunteering.

Take part. Respond. Build

For more information, email cbve@riovoluntario.org.br

Extracted from <http://www.riovoluntario.org.br/blog/index.php?cat=77&paged=2>. Accessed on October 28, 2009.

corporate volunteering: voluntariado empresarial
performed: realizado

survey: pesquisa
take part: participe

After Reading

1 Answer the questions.

a What kinds of businesses can take part in the survey?

_____

b What is the main goal of the survey?

_____

c What do companies have to do if they decide to participate?

_____

d How can people find more information about the survey?

_____

2 Write T (true) or F (false). Correct and rewrite the false sentences.

a (   ) Our country needs to know about corporate volunteering.

_____

_____

b (   ) Responding to the survey won't cause changes in corporate volunteering.

_____

_____

c (   ) There haven't been many large studies like this before.

_____

_____

3 Read the sentence below and check the correct alternatives.

"[...] Corporate volunteerism can be a triple win: helping people in the community while giving employees a chance to shine and benefiting the company in numerous ways."

Source: Minnesota Council on Foundations.
Extracted from <http://www.minnesotagiving.org/options/corpvol.htm>.
Accessed on October 28, 2009.

a (   ) Everybody can win with corporate volunteering.

b (   ) Employees are not involved in this project.

c (   ) Employees can do things they are good at.

d (   ) The community is the only one to benefit from corporate volunteering.

e (   ) Companies are never involved in volunteering.

4 Leia o extrato de texto abaixo e discuta-o com seus colegas.

"As ONG's (organizações não governamentais) são organizações formadas pela sociedade civil sem fins lucrativos e que têm como missão a resolução de algum problema da sociedade, seja ele econômico, racial, ambiental, etc., ou ainda a reivindicação de direitos, melhorias e fiscalização do poder público. [...]"

Extraído de <http://www.infoescola.com/geografia/ongs-organizacoes-nao-governamentais>.
Acessado em 30 de março de 2010.
Autora: Caroline Ferreira.

a O que as organizações não governamentais têm em comum com o voluntariado empresarial?

b De quais ONGs você já ouviu falar?

c Você teria interesse em participar de projetos voluntários? Quais?

Vocabulary in Use

1 The word *volunteer* has different meanings, including all those listed below. Check the meanings that are used in the text "Corporate Volunteering Survey in Brazil" on page 44. You can choose more than one alternative.

a (   ) To offer or choose to do something without being forced.

b (   ) To say something, or to give information without being asked.

c (   ) To agree to join the armed forces without being forced.

d (   ) To do some work without getting paid.

e (   ) To say that someone else will do something before asking them if they are willing to do it.

2 The words in the box **are not** related to the meanings of *volunteer*. Find them in the crossword.

forced	obligated	paid	salaried	unwilling

G	Y	L	P	P	A	S	O	F	Q
R	H	Y	Q	A	M	J	B	L	G
O	G	T	K	D	B	N	L	T	S
A	U	N	W	I	L	L	I	N	G
P	F	O	R	C	E	D	G	B	G
S	Q	U	H	E	D	G	A	N	M
A	E	P	I	O	G	T	T	C	A
K	S	A	L	A	R	I	E	D	A
W	K	I	I	T	Y	L	D	X	A
R	E	D	T	Y	U	A	Q	L	I

Reprodução proibida. Art.184 do Código Penal e Lei 9.610 de 19 de fevereiro de 1998

3 Complete the sentences below with the words in exercise 2. Use the glossary if necessary.

a The differences between _____ and hourly employees are set by federal laws.

b She is _____ to sit with us and discuss the project.

c The employees were _____ for their work.

d I didn't want to tell them about that. I was _____ to.

e Please, don't _____ us to do this job. We hate it.

Grammar in Use

PRESENT PERFECT

FORMAÇÃO: **HAVE/HAS** + PARTICÍPIO PASSADO DO VERBO PRINCIPAL	
Forma afirmativa	Several companies **have responded** to the CBVE survey. Your company **has taken** part in a volunteering project.
Forma negativa	Unfortunately, volunteering **hasn't become** a habit in Brazil. Many industries **haven't motivated** their employees to work on behalf of others.
Forma interrogativa	**A: Have** you **helped** any charitable organizations? **B:** Yes, I have. / No, I haven't. **A: Has** she **gained** experience through volunteering? **B:** Yes, she has. / No, she hasn't.
Formas abreviadas	**'ve** = have **'s** = has **haven't** = have not **hasn't** = has not

USO	
O **Present Perfect** é utilizado para indicar ações que aconteceram em um passado indefinido. Essas ações podem ter terminado ou ainda estar ocorrendo.	I have studied English here for ten years.
Pode ser usado com:	
• **Since** (desde)	I have known him **since** 1990.
• **For** (por)	They haven't been married **for** so long.
• **Just** (recentemente)	I can smell her perfume in the air. She has **just** left.
• **Ever** (alguma vez, já)	Have you **ever** traveled abroad?
• **Never** (nunca)	They have **never** tried Japanese food.
• **Already** (já)	Summer has **already** begun.
• **Yet** (ainda, já)	I left my CV at the store but they haven't called me for an interview **yet**. Has your mom heard the good news **yet**?
• **Lately, recently** (ultimamente, recentemente)	We haven't seen her in the neighborhood **recently**. Has she moved away?
• **Many times** (muitas vezes)	Has the little boy visited his grandma **many times** this month?

1 Match the photos to the sentences.

YING GENG / SHUTTERSTOCK

(A)

AFP / GETTY IMAGES

(B)

TOMAS LOUTOCKY / SHUTTERSTOCK

(C)

KEITH NEALE / MASTERFILE / OTHER IMAGES

(D)

HERVÉ GYSSELS / PHOTONONSTOP / IMAGEPLUS

(E)

( ) The doctor has prescribed some medicine to the man.

( ) Have the flowers blossomed?

( ) He hasn't won the championship but he has won the race.

( ) Have they bought a new camera?

( ) The maid hasn't cleaned the house yet.

2 Unscramble the words to make questions. Use the Present Perfect. Then complete the short answers.

TIP

O *Past Participle* dos verbos regulares e de alguns irregulares (ver lista na página 181) tem a mesma forma do *Simple Past*.

a Mexico / ever / been to / Have / you

A: _____

B: Yes, _____.

b known / mom and dad / 20 years / Have / each other / for

A: _____

B: Yes, _____.

c   the boy / yet / for the test / Has / studied

A: _____

B: No, _____.

d   lately / bought / you / DVDs / Have

A: _____

B: No, _____.

e   the latest news / Has / heard / just / she

A: _____

B: Yes, _____.

3 Choose the best alternative.

3.1 I have _____ answered my e-mails.

a ( ) already   b ( ) since   c ( ) many times

3.2 You haven't come to my place _____ August.

a ( ) for   b ( ) since   c ( ) just

3.3 Susan has _____ arrived from school.

a ( ) for   b ( ) yet   c ( ) just

3.4 They haven't handed in their projects _____.

a ( ) yet   b ( ) already   c ( ) never

3.5 Have we _____ met?

a ( ) ever   b ( ) since   c ( ) many times

3.6 Has it occurred to you that the poor boy has _____ had a chance in life?

a ( ) since   b ( ) ever   c ( ) never

4 Write the sentences below in the negative and interrogative forms.

a   The dentist has provided teeth cleaning.

_____

_____

b   Teachers have taught adult lessons in the community.

_____

_____

c   The housewife has babysat other women's children.

_____

_____

5 Complete part of the song "We Are the Champions" by Queen with the verbs in the box. Use the Present Perfect.

be	come	do	have	make	pay	take

I _____ my dues

Time after time

I _____ my sentence

But committed no crime

And bad mistakes

I'_____ a few

I'_____ my share of sand

Kicked in my face

But I'_____ through

And I need to go on and on and on and on

We are the champions my friends

And we'll keep on fighting till the end

We are the champions

We are the champions

No time for losers

'Cause we are the champions of the world

I'_____ my bows

And my curtain calls

You brought me fame and fortune

And everything that goes with it

I thank you all

But it'_____ no bed of roses

No pleasure cruise

I consider it a challenge before

The whole human race

And I ain't gonna lose

And I need to go on and on and on and on

[...]

"EMI" – EMI Songs do Brasil Edições Musicais Ltda.
Extracted from <http://letras.terra.com.br/queen>.
Accessed on February 11, 2010.

Reading

File   Edit   View   Favorites   Tools   Help

Address http://www.workingabroad.com/page/192/volunteer-brazil-details.htm

Media and Design Innovation

Help to link the people of Brazil to global opportunities through technology.

Brazil is one of the most rapidly developing economies in the world. Dubbed one of the world's leading developing countries, Brazil is fast becoming a powerhouse of business, industry, and innovation. Unfortunately, many people from Brazil's favelas (or urban slums) have limited access to the opportunities the country's emerging economy offers. That's why this program has expanded opportunities for people who live in favelas – working to give them increased access to opportunities across Brazil.

Technology is the key to the global economy, and it's the goal of many of our partner NGOs to empower people from the favelas to learn how to use technology so they can have access to these emerging opportunities in Brazil. As a volunteer in a technological innovation program, you may help teach people of all ages to use technology, set up new systems at partner program sites, and/or maintain and upgrade existing systems to support new technologies.

Only basic technological proficiency is necessary to work on a technology program – i.e. knowing the basic functions of operating systems like Microsoft Office. However should you be interested to offer specialist skills in technology, please let us know and a tailored program can be devised accordingly.

[...]

How to Get Involved?

If you are interested in joining this project, you will need to fill out the online application form (you can also print it out and send it to us by post) – to secure a placement on the project, please complete and submit the form including two references and your deposit of £180. If for some reason, your application is declined, we will reimburse this deposit fully. However for those who are accepted, the full amount needs to be paid in Brazilian reals upon arrival (due to currency fluctuations). Once we have confirmed your place, you will receive a pre-departure package with all detailed information on your project, Rio de Janeiro, suggested items to bring, etc.

Start

Extracted from <http://www.workingabroad.com/page/192/volunteer-brazil-details.htm>.
Accessed on November 4, 2009.

declined: recusado
devised: criado, projetado
dubbed: conhecido
emerging: em desenvolvimento
empower: capacitar, habilitar
goal: objetivo
powerhouse: fonte de influência

pre-departure package: conjunto de programas enviado antes da partida
reimburse: reembolsaremos
secure: garantir
set up: criar, estabelecer
submit: submeter
tailored: adaptado

After Reading

1 Read the statements and mark True, False or Not Mentioned according to the text on page 51.

	True	False	Not Mentioned
a Brazil has considerable influence over the global economy nowadays.	( )	( )	( )
b The number of people who live in slums is growing every year.	( )	( )	( )
c Technology can help people from Brazil's slums to get equal opportunities.	( )	( )	( )
d Previous experience is required to work on a technology program.	( )	( )	( )
e If your application is not accepted, the agency will not give your money back.	( )	( )	( )

2 The sentence below has been extracted from the text on page 44. Read it again and pay close attention to the expression in bold.

> "Large, medium, small, and micro businesses should **take part** in this survey."

The expression in bold is a collocation. What is a collocation? Read below.

> **collocation** the way in which some words are often used together, or a particular combination of words.

Longman Dictionary of Contemporary English. London: Longman, 2003. 4th ed. p. 1259.

Appendix 3
page 165

Fill in the gaps with the appropriate collocation.

a She _____ on the interviewer. That's why she got the job.

b You can _____ in your community if you do volunteering work.

c There are lots of plates and glasses in the kitchen sink. Dad needs help to

_____.

d The annual event of the volunteering project will _____

in Curitiba.

e Some companies _____ with small farmers from the countryside of Brazil.

f _____ and study harder for the finals.

3 Read the dictionary entry and do the activity.

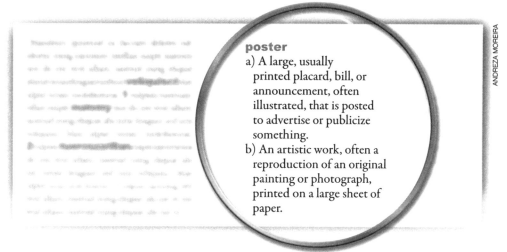

poster
a) A large, usually printed placard, bill, or announcement, often illustrated, that is posted to advertise or publicize something.
b) An artistic work, often a reproduction of an original painting or photograph, printed on a large sheet of paper.

Extracted from <http://dictionary.reference.com/browse/poster>.
Accessed on February 1, 2010.

Os pôsteres têm como principais características: letras grandes, presença de mapas ou ilustrações, sequência de itens, *layout* apelativo e posição das informações no papel para facilitar a leitura. Leia novamente o pôster da página 44 e responda às questões abaixo.

a O pôster apresenta título? Você acha que o título é atraente? Por quê? / Por que não?

_____

_____

b De onde o pôster foi extraído?

_____

_____

c Com que intenção esse texto foi escrito?

_____

_____

d Quem são os prováveis leitores desse pôster?

_____

_____

e Quais das características apresentadas são encontradas no pôster?

_____

_____

Language in Action

Reprodução proibida. Art.184 do Código Penal e Lei 9.610 de 19 de fevereiro de 1998.

TIP Não tente entender cada palavra que você escuta. Procure entender palavras importantes no contexto.

1 Listen to an environmental engineer talking about what some people have done to preserve the environment. Write the names of the people who have done the actions below.

a _____ collected almost 60 pounds of trash near their school

b _____ cleaned up a creek in their neighborhood

c _____ raised salmon from eggs until they were big enough to be released into a stream

d _____ cleaned up a playground in their neighborhood

e _____ planted trees in a neighborhood park to celebrate National Arbor Day

2 Some problems are the same all over the world, no matter where people live. Some of these problems are illustrated below. Talk to a classmate about them. Use the suggestions in the box to help you.

> fundraise to build houses   recycle   start a campaign for food donations
> teach computer / language / art / music

A: What can we do to solve the problem of garbage on streets?
B: Well, we can recycle the garbage.

garbage on streets

homelessness

child labor

hunger

54

Now, talk to a classmate about the problems faced in your community.
What can you do to solve them? You can use a dictionary if necessary.

Picture Dictionary 3

page 158

Writing

Join in small groups and **create a poster on a volunteering** project.

- Decide who your **target audience is and where** the poster is going to be placed: in your classroom or **outside the school.**

- Think of a slogan.

- On a separate piece of **thick paper, write down** the slogan at the top.

- Then write down **sentences to encourage people** to do any kind of volunteer work. You can use the **words and expressions** studied in this unit.

- Paste photos or **do drawings to illustrate** the poster.

- Use the space below to **draft your poster.**

PHOTO: MALEWITCH / SHUTTERSTOCK; ART. RAFAEL GENTILE

Consultando outras fontes

filmes: *A corrente do bem* (EUA, 2000; direção: Mimi Leder)
Patch Adams, o amor é contagioso (EUA, 1998; direção: Tom Shadyac)

livro: *O trabalho voluntário* (Senac Editora; autora: Maria Cristina Dal Rio)

Social Worker

A social worker is in charge of planning and executing public policies and social projects that aim for everybody's welfare. They evaluate and report the situation a person, a family, or a community is in – and if one of them is in any kind of risk it is the social worker's job to propose an action that will make the condition better. These professionals support the development of communities and minorities, as well as fight against social injustice, in an attempt to integrate everyone into a unified society. Another part of a social worker's job is to oversee adoption, making sure that the child to be adopted is going to be in good hands and that the whole process – including the paperwork – is done correctly.

Social workers can do their job in public institutions, such as hospitals, health centers, jails, shelters, among many others. They can also take part in a private company's human resources team, which will give them the opportunity to tend to employees' personal issues and prevent accidents in the workplace. However, the area where you have the best chance of being hired as a social worker is the health industry.

Becoming a social worker involves taking a four-year course, as well as supervised apprenticeships and registration in the Regional Social Workers' Council.

Based on <http://www.jobprofiles.org/programs/health-medical/social-work.htm>; <http://www.nhscareers.nhs.uk/details/Default.aspx?Id=519>; <http://education-portal.com/search/quicksearch.html>. Accessed on January 30, 2010.

employees: funcionários
in charge of: encarregado de
paperwork: papelada
policies: políticas
shelters: abrigos

support: apoiam
tend to: cuidar de
unified: unificada
welfare: bem-estar

Para mais informações, acesse:

<http://guiadoestudante.abril.com.br/profissoes/ciencias-humanas-sociais/profissoes_280104.shtml>;

<http://www.infoescola.com/profissoes/assistente-social>;

<http://www.brasilprofissoes.com.br/verprof.php?codigo=64>.

1 Você gostaria de ser assistente social? Por quê? / Por que não?

2 The photos below show some of the things a social worker usually does.
Match them to the situations they refer to.

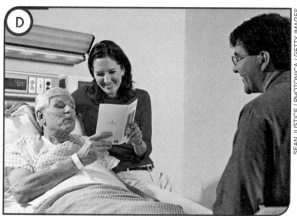

( ) Disabled people are applying for access to public means of transportation.

( ) All the families in the neighborhood are rebuilding their houses after the flood.

( ) After the heart surgery, Mr. Todd and his family need information about how to get over it.

( ) The company needs someone able to hire some technicians.

( ) The judge wants a report about how the adopted child is living.

Additional Practice

For exercises 1 to 8, choose the best alternative.

1 The workers have been talking for hours, but no decision has been made _____.

a ( ) ever
b ( ) never
c ( ) already
d ( ) just
e ( ) yet

2 A: Who's that guy over there? Do you know him?

B: That's Paulo. I've known him _____ 2005.

a ( ) for
b ( ) since
c ( ) just
d ( ) yet
e ( ) never

3 A: I really want to try that new Japanese restaurant. Would you like to go with me?

B: Sorry, but I don't like Japanese food.

A: How do you know that if you have _____ tried it before?

a ( ) lately
b ( ) recently
c ( ) many times
d ( ) never
e ( ) ever

4 A: Are you already working in that company?

B: No, I left my CV there, but they _____ me yet.

a ( ) have called
b ( ) haven't call
c ( ) haven't called
d ( ) has called
e ( ) hasn't called

5 "Google today announced that daily YouTube uploads directly from mobile devices _____ 400% since the release of the iPhone 3GS last Friday. […]"

Extracted from <http://www.macrumors.com/.../ youtube-daily-mobile-uploads-have-increased>. Accessed on February 13, 2010.

a ( ) has increased
b ( ) have increased
c ( ) haven't increased
d ( ) hasn't increased
e ( ) had increased

6 Which sentence means that Tyler still works at the company?

a ( ) Tyler worked here for 4 years.
b ( ) Tyler is going to work here for 4 years.
c ( ) Tyler hasn't worked here for 4 years.
d ( ) Tyler can work here for 4 years.
e ( ) Tyler has worked here for 4 years.

7 The students want to know how to _____ in a volunteering program to help the victims of the flood.

a ( ) survey
b ( ) perform
c ( ) take part
d ( ) empower
e ( ) secure

8 The meeting of psychologists this semester will _____ at the university auditorium.

a ( ) take place

b ( ) take part

c ( ) make a difference

d ( ) make impression on

e ( ) take a chance

9 If you want to meet your bigger _____, take small steps. When you take things slowly, you'll see progress faster.

a ( ) empower

b ( ) secure

c ( ) goal

d ( ) dubbed

e ( ) emerge

10 Choose the alternative that best completes this part of the lyrics of "Anybody Seen my baby?", by The Rolling Stones.

Salty tears

It's three in the afternoon

_____

Is she really gone for good?

a ( ) Has she disappeared?

b ( ) She has disappeared?

c ( ) She disappeared?

d ( ) She have disappeared?

e ( ) Has disappeared she?

Refletindo sobre sua aprendizagem

Ao final desta unidade, você já é capaz de:

- Fazer leitura de pôsteres, refletir sobre eles e confrontar as opiniões com as informações contidas nas imagens e no texto. ☐
- Localizar informações específicas no texto, analisá-las e corrigi-las, se necessário. ☐
- Expressar pontos de vista em relação ao voluntariado e discutir com os colegas da sala e com o professor possibilidades e ações. ☐
- Associar o significado de uma palavra ao contexto em que ela se encontra. ☐
- Identificar palavras pertencentes ao mesmo campo semântico e usá-las em diferentes contextos. ☐
- Reconhecer o emprego e a função comunicativa de verbos no *Present Perfect*. ☐
- Produzir frases afirmativas e negativas com marcadores de tempo. ☐
- Reconhecer o significado de algumas *collocations* em diferentes situações comunicativas. ☐
- Fazer levantamento dos problemas da comunidade e buscar soluções para eles. ☐
- Produzir um pôster. ☐

Aprimorando sua aprendizagem

- Peça ajuda ao professor ou aos colegas para que esclareçam suas dúvidas.
- Refaça os exercícios.
- Visite a biblioteca da sua escola ou uma biblioteca pública e consulte livros de gramática e/ou faça leituras de seu interesse.
- Assista a filmes em inglês.

PRE-READING
Look at the photos. Do you know who these people are?

"I learned that courage was not the absence of fear, but the triumph over it. The brave man is not he who does not feel afraid, but he who conquers that fear."

Nelson Mandela, South-African president (1994-1999)
1994 inaugural speech

Extracted from <http://www.quotesdaddy.com/quote/986740/nelson-mandela/
i-learned-that-courage-was-not-the-absence-of-fear>.
Accessed on February 8, 2010.

*"It was a creed written into the founding documents that declared the destiny of a nation.
Yes we can.
It was whispered by slaves and abolitionists as they blazed a trail
towards freedom through the darkest of nights.
Yes we can.
It was sung by immigrants as they struck out from distant shores and pioneers
who pushed westward against an unforgiving wilderness.
Yes we can."*

Barack Obama, 44th president of United States
New Hampshire Democratic Primary speech – January 8, 2009.

Extracted from <http://www.quotationspage.com/quote/40438.html>.
Accessed on Febuary 8, 2010.

*"At first I thought I was fighting to save rubber trees,
then I thought I was fighting to save the Amazon rainforest.
Now I realize I am fighting for humanity."*

Chico Mendes (1944-1988), a Brazilian environmental activist and union leader

Extracted from <http://www.unep.org/billiontreecampaign/Treeandhumanity/index.asp>.
Accessed on February 8, 2010.

*"Brazil is Paradise for a minority, Purgatory for most people,
and Hell for 20 percent of the population."*

Herbert de Souza, an activist against economic injustice and government corruption
in an interview for *New Internationalist* magazine, February 1995

Extracted from <http://www.newint.org/issue264/interview.htm>.
Accessed on February 8, 2010.

absence: ausência	**fear:** medo	**slaves:** escravos
blazed: marcaram com chamas	**hell:** inferno	**speech:** discurso
creed: prece	**purgatory:** purgatório	**whispered:** sussurrado

After Reading

1 Read the quotations on page 60 again and complete the statements below.

   a Mandela's inaugural speech was _____.

   b Obama's speech was _____, in _____.

   c Chico Mendes was born _____ and died _____.

   d Herbert de Souza's interview was for _____.

2 Write synonyms for the words in bold. Use the words given.

> fate
> fright
> heaven
> notice
> belief

   a "I learned that courage was not the absence of **fear** [...]" _____

   b "It was a **creed** written into the founding documents [...]" _____

   c "[...] that declared the **destiny** of a nation." _____

   d "Now I **realize** I am fighting for humanity." _____

   e "Brazil is **Paradise** for a minority [...]" _____

3 Answer the questions below in Portuguese.

   a What did Mandela mean by "I learned that courage was not the absence of fear, but the triumph over it"?

   _____

   _____

   b In Obama's speech, who fought for freedom?

   _____

   _____

   c What were the rubber trees Chico Mendes referred to in his speech?

   _____

   d Herbert de Souza compared Brazil to Paradise, Purgatory, and Hell. What did he mean?

   _____

   _____

Vocabulary in Use

1 Complete the sentences below with the linking words given.

> **and:** e   **afterwards:** depois disso   **before:** antes
>
> **but:** mas   **in the end:** por fim   **like:** como
>
> **such as:** tal como, tais como   **then:** então

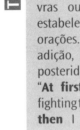

Linking words são palavras ou expressões que estabelecem ligações entre orações. Podem indicar adição, contraste, causa, posteridade, etc.
"**At first** I thought I was fighting to save rubber trees, **then** I thought I was..."

a There is no help for those with lots of luggage _____ packages.

b Cartoon characters _____ Monica and Smudge are still popular.

c It wasn't that he lied, exactly, _____ he did tend to exaggerate.

d _____ they decided to buy the cheapest house.

e Life was harder _____ because neither of us had a job.

f She offended her sister. _____, she begged for forgiveness.

g Put your money in a safe place _____ it gets stolen.

h It didn't turn out _____ I had intended.

2 Read an extract from the book *True Heroes of Sport* by Donatella Fitzgerald. This book is about a famous baseball player called Babe Ruth. Fill in the gaps with linking words.

"[...] George's mother and father worked long hours and didn't have much time for him, _____ he played out in the street all day. _____ he was seven, he went to live at Saint Mary's, a school for boys. _____ his parents took him home from time to time, _____ in the end he went to live at Saint Mary's all the time. His parents never visited him there.

At Saint Mary's one of his teacher was Brother Mathias. Mathias became young George's friend _____ taught him to play baseball. George _____ became a very good player. When he was only nineteen, he began playing professionally with the Baltimore Orioles. _____ he was very young, the players in the team called him "Babe" and _____ "Babe Ruth" became his name. [...]"

Extracted from *True Heroes of Sport*, Donatella Fitzgerald,
Oxford University Press, 2002, 6th edition, page 4.

Appendix 4

page 166

Grammar in Use

PRESENT PERFECT x SIMPLE PAST

O **Simple Past** refere-se a ações totalmente concluídas no tempo passado.	What Mandela **said** about courage **in 1994** is still true.
Já o **Present Perfect** refere-se a ações iniciadas no passado que ainda podem estar em andamento no presente, ou que ocorreram no passado, mas não podemos precisar quando.	Chico Mendes **has taught** the world how important it is to preserve the Amazon.

1 Underline the correct verb form in the dialogues below.

a **Yvonne:** How long **have you been** / **were you** a nutrition technician?

Simon: Well, I **got** / **have gotten** my first job when I was 21, so I **am** / **have been** a nutrition technician for five years now.

b **Sarah: Did you visit** / **Have you visited** Montreal when you were in Canada for the first time?

Raymond: No, I couldn't. There was a bad snow storm at that time. But I **visited** / **have visited** Montreal twice since then.

c **Sophia:** William **has brought** / **brought** Zoe some fruit and magazines when he came to see her.

George: That was very nice of him.

2 Rearrange the words to form 5 sentences. The first one is done for you.

whenever	they	passed	where	yet?
have	haven't	her	this movie	on the counter
she	you	walked past	purse	she was?
we	someone	seen	the gate	exam?
did	left	know	the	the dog barked

She left her purse on the counter.

_____

_____

_____

_____

_____

3 Read an extract from the book *The Adventures of Huckleberry Finn* by Mark Twain and fill in the gaps with the verbs in parentheses. Use the Simple Past or the Present Perfect. You can use the list of irregular verbs on page 181 to help you.

"[…] Jim _____ (hid) in the hut and _____ (start) to move the raft out into the current again. But after a moment, I _____ (hear) somebody shouting to me. I _____ (look) round.

Two white men were paddling a boat towards us. They _____ (stop) their boat near the raft. One of them _____ (speak) to me.

"_____ you _____ (see) any black men here, boy?" he said.

"Five slaves _____ (escape) from a farm near here. There's a reward for them."

"No," I _____ (say). "I _____ (see) any black men."

"Are there *any* men in the hut on your raft?" he asked.

"There's – there's one man, sir," I _____ (answer). "My father is in there."

The man _____ (believe) me. […]"

RAFAEL GENTILE

Extracted from *The Adventures of Huckleberry Finn*, Mark Twain, Macmillan Heinemann ELT, 2005, 3rd edition, page 32.

PRESENT PERFECT CONTINUOUS

FORMAÇÃO: **HAVE/HAS BEEN** + VERBO PRINCIPAL + **ING**

Forma afirmativa	Barack Obama **has been working** as a community activist since his youth.
Forma negativa	Barack Obama **hasn't been working** as a community activist since his youth.
Forma interrogativa	**A: Has** Barack Obama **been working** as a community activist since his youth? **B:** Yes, he has. / No, he hasn't.
Formas abreviadas	**'s** = has **hasn't** = has not **haven't** = have not

USO

O **Present Perfect Continuous** é utilizado para expressar uma ação iniciada no passado e que ainda está em progresso por um período de tempo não específico. É frequentemente usado com *how long* para fazer perguntas e com *for*, *since* e *lately* nas formas afirmativas.	**A:** How long has the politician been leading the country? **B:** He has been leading the country **for** 5 years.

4 What has Garfield been doing lately? Look at the picture, read the sentences and write T (true) or F (false).

a ( ) He hasn't been cleaning his room.

b ( ) He has been drinking cola.

c ( ) He has been surfing the web.

d ( ) He has been reading the newspaper.

e ( ) He hasn't been tiding his drawers.

5 Read the dialogues below. Fill in the gaps using the Present Perfect or the Present Perfect Continuous. Use the verbs given.

a **A:** _____ you ever _____ (meet) a movie star?
B: Not really, but I _____ (work) for a country singer since last year.

b **A:** Where _____ you _____ (be)? We _____ (wait) for you since noon.
B: Sorry, I was at the hairstylist.

c **A:** Anna, _____ Sarah _____ (read) any of Machado de Assis's novels?
B: Sure. She _____ (read) *Dom Casmurro* since last weekend.

6 Ask questions using *How long.* Use *for* and *since* to answer them. The first one is done for you.

They / dance / 2 hours

A: How long have they been dancing?
B: They have been dancing for 2 hours.

Erick / take / the exam / early in the morning

_____

_____

The Tomikos / take a vacation / for 20 days

_____

_____

Miss Hill's dogs / cause trouble in the neighborhood / last year

_____

_____

7 Answer the questions below about yourself.

a Where and when were you born?

_____

b What did you use to do on weekends when you were a child?

_____

c Have you ever been to a museum? Which one?

_____

d Have you ever practiced any sports?

_____

e How long have you been studying in this school?

_____

Reading

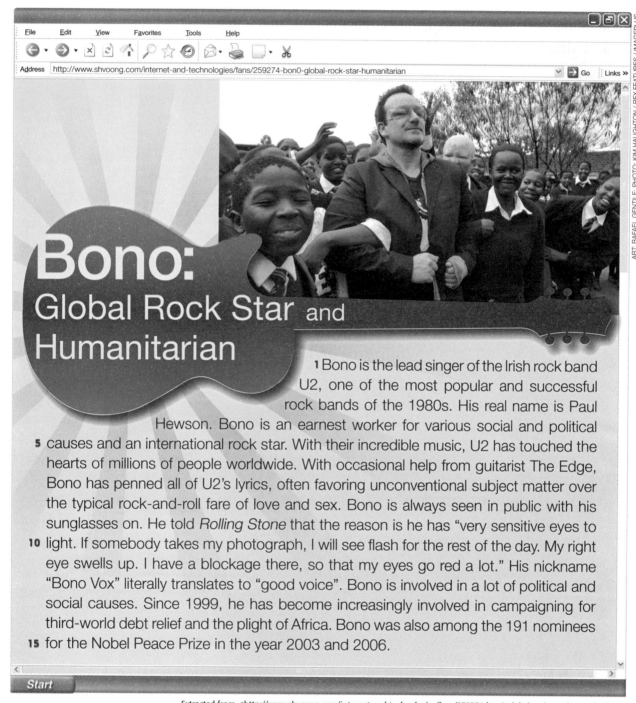

File   Edit   View   Favorites   Tools   Help

Address http://www.shvoong.com/internet-and-technologies/fans/259274-bon0-global-rock-star-humanitarian   Go   Links »

Bono:
Global Rock Star and
Humanitarian

1 Bono is the lead singer of the Irish rock band U2, one of the most popular and successful rock bands of the 1980s. His real name is Paul Hewson. Bono is an earnest worker for various social and political

5 causes and an international rock star. With their incredible music, U2 has touched the hearts of millions of people worldwide. With occasional help from guitarist The Edge, Bono has penned all of U2's lyrics, often favoring unconventional subject matter over the typical rock-and-roll fare of love and sex. Bono is always seen in public with his sunglasses on. He told *Rolling Stone* that the reason is he has "very sensitive eyes to

10 light. If somebody takes my photograph, I will see flash for the rest of the day. My right eye swells up. I have a blockage there, so that my eyes go red a lot." His nickname "Bono Vox" literally translates to "good voice". Bono is involved in a lot of political and social causes. Since 1999, he has become increasingly involved in campaigning for third-world debt relief and the plight of Africa. Bono was also among the 191 nominees

15 for the Nobel Peace Prize in the year 2003 and 2006.

Start

Extracted from <http://www.shvoong.com/internet-and-technologies/fans/259274-bon0-global-rock-star-humanitarian>.
Accessed on November 4, 2009.

Picture Dictionary 4
page 159

blockage: obstrução
campaigning: fazer campanha
lead: principal
nominees: pessoas nomeadas

sensitive: sensíveis
subject matter: tema
worldwide: por todo o mundo

After Reading

1 Read the text about Bono again. Write the numbers of the lines where you can find the following information.

a The meaning of "Bono Vox". (_____)

b Bono's choice of using unusual themes in U2's songs. (_____)

c Bono's latest contribution to the world. (_____)

d The reason why Bono always wears sunglasses. (_____)

2 Choose the right word to complete each sentence below. You can find all the words in the text on the previous page.

2.1 Doctor Ross studied the laws for days and finally he proved the innocence of the woman. He is a very _____ man.

   a ( ) social

   b ( ) earnest

   c ( ) political

2.2 Mário de Andrade is the author of *Pauliceia Desvairada*. It was _____ in 1922.

   a ( ) penned

   b ( ) involved

   c ( ) touched

2.3 Yesterday I looked for a doctor because I had a terrible headache. At the doctor's office my eyes _____, so I couldn't drive back home.

   a ( ) became

   b ( ) seen

   c ( ) swelled up

2.4 Whenever I talked about his past life, he would _____.

   a ( ) feel blue

   b ( ) go red

   c ( ) be in black and white

2.5 The _____ of Haitians after the earthquake touched everybody's heart all over the world.

   a ( ) lead

   b ( ) plight

   c ( ) light

3 In Book 1 (Unit 4) we learned that a biography is a short text about somebody whose life is very important or interesting. Sometimes quotations are used in biographies to make the narrative more vivid and convincing. Read the dictionary entry below and do the activity.

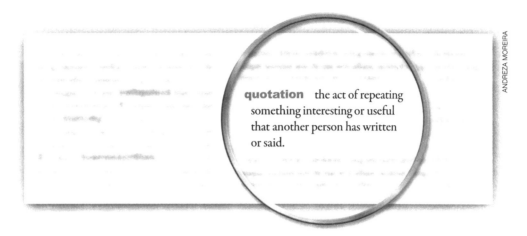

quotation the act of repeating something interesting or useful that another person has written or said.

Oxford Advanced Learner's Dictionary. 7th edition. Oxford: Oxford University, 2005. page 1239.

The quotations below were said by the same people mentioned on page 60. Read the quotations and identify who said each of them.

a "If a messenger from the sky came down and guaranteed that my death would strengthen our struggle, it would be worth it. But experience teaches us the contrary. It's not with big funerals and motions of support that we're going to save the Amazon. I want to live."

_____

b "When students participate in debate, they learn to study issues in depth and from all perspectives, a skill I use every day in the Senate."

_____

c "We either have to definitively accept that poverty and misery are part of our culture and therefore consolidate our social apartheid. Or we have to review our history, our vision of the world. There is no reason, no argument, no theory that justifies the existence of this misery."

_____

d "I have fought against white domination, and I have fought against black domination. I have cherished the ideal of a democratic and free society in which all persons live together in harmony and with equal opportunities. It is an ideal which I hope to live for and to achieve. But if needs be, it is an ideal for which I am prepared to die."

_____

Extracted from <http://www.fragilecologies.com/apr26_99.html>;
<http://news.egypt.com/en/news/us-presidential-election/barack-obama-quotes-4.html>;
<http://www.nytimes.com/1993/06/06/weekinreview/conversations-herbert-jose-de-souza-hard-look-brazil-s-surfeits-food-hunger>html?pagewanted=1>;
<http://www.nelsonmandela.org/index.php/news/article/making_peace_marks_40th_anniversary_of_albert_luthulis_death>.
Acessed on February 20, 2010.

ANDREZA MOREIRA

Language in Action

1 Jonathan Cox is a journalist from Missouri. Once a week he listens to a radio program about icons that have been admired because of their ideas. Using pieces of information he hears on the radio, he writes his articles. Listen to part of the program about Mahatma Gandhi that Jonathan listened to last week and underline the correct words.

Gandhi, the pioneer of non-violence, believed in simplicity. His simple attire became a subject of great **contemplation / constellation** and ridicule in Western nations. His compelling ideas braved death and continued to be a source of **transpiration / inspiration** and emulation for great leaders like Martin Luther King Jr., Cesar Chavez, and Nelson Mandela. Here are some famous words from Gandhi.

[...]

Attitude

Be the **change / chance** you want to see in the world.

Love

Whenever you are confronted with an **opponent / component**, conquer him with love.

[...]

Happiness

Happiness is when what you **thing / think**, what you say, and what you do are in harmony.

Forgiveness

Hate / Date the sin, love the sinner.

[...]

Non-violence

Non-violence is a weapon of the strong.

[...]

Source: *Kids Portal for Parents*
Extracted from <http://www.4to40.com/culture/print.asp?id=292>.
Accessed on January 18, 2010.

2 Jonathan Cox is talking to his coworker Margaret about the icons that were presented in the last radio programs. Read their dialogue. In pairs make new dialogues. Use the cues given.

Margaret: What program did you like best?

Jonathan: To me, the one about Gandhi was the best.

Margaret: Why?

Jonathan: Because he was the pioneer of non-violence and believed in simplicity.

A	B
Barack Obama Chico Mendes Gandhi Nelson Mandela Herbert de Souza Bono Vox	was the first black president in the U.S. fought for humanitarian causes protected the rainforests fought against prejudice was the pioneer of non-violence and believed in simplicity was involved in political and social causes

3 Now it's your turn!

Ask a classmate who his or her icon is and why. Talk about people who were not mentioned in this unit.

Writing

The radio program broadcaster Mr. Morgan has asked listeners to suggest who they would like the next programs to be about. Jonathan Cox has decided to write a letter and suggest a name. If you were a journalist, who would you suggest? Complete the letter below justifying your suggestion. Use a dictionary if necessary.

RAFAEL GENTILE

_____ (place)
_____ (date)

Dear Mr. Morgan,

_____ (your name and occupation)

I have heard you are looking for suggestions on who we would like the next programs to be about.

I would like to hear about _____ because

_____

_____

I look forward to receiving a positive response from you soon.
Sincerely,

_____ (name)

Consultando outras fontes

filme: *Pelé Eterno* (Brasil, 2004, documentário; direção: Aníbal Massaini Neto)

livros: *Barack Obama – A origem dos Meus Sonhos* (Gente, 2008; autor: Barack Obama)

Einstein – Sua Vida, seu Universo (Companhia das Letras, 2007; autor: Walter Isaacson)

True Heroes of Sport (Oxford do Brasil, 2002; autora: Donatella Fitzgerald)

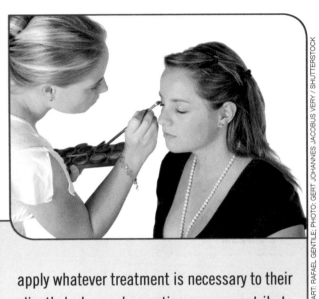

 # Personal-Appearance Professional

A lot of people say that what matters most in a person is what's inside, and not the way he or she looks. However, as much as some people try to deny it, physical image is very important — especially when it comes to first impressions. So, in order to make the best first impression possible, you can always count on the help of a personal-appearance professional.

These professionals are in charge of making a person look as good as he or she possibly can. In order to do so, they must know exactly what kind of haircut and makeup will compliment the person's features, as well as the occasion they're preparing for. They are also supposed to apply whatever treatment is necessary to their client's looks, and sometimes even contribute to forming a character for plays, movies, and soap operas.

A personal-appearance professional can work for beauty parlors, spas, hotels — basically any place where beauty treatments are offered. He or she may also work with cosmetic, beauty, and fashion companies, or have his or her own business.

In order to become a personal-appearance professional, you have to take an 800-hour course (approximately 18 months).

Based on <http://www.bls.gov/oco/ocos332.htm>; <http://www.wisegeek.com/what-is-an-image-consultancy.htm>; <http://online.onetcenter.org/link/summary/39-5012.00>; <http://www.careerplanner.com/Job-Outlook/Barbers-Cosmetologists-and-Other-Personal-Appearance-Workers.cfm>. Accessed on February 5, 2010.

beauty parlors: salões de beleza
deny: negar
features: atributos, traços
haircut: corte de cabelo
in charge of: responsáveis por
soap operas: novelas

Para mais informações, acesse:

<http://catalogonct.mec.gov.br/et_ambiente_saude_seguranca/t_imagem_pessoal.php>;

<http://www.centropaulasouza.sp.gov.br/Cursos/ETE/imagem-pessoal.html>.

1 Você gostaria de ser técnico em imagem pessoal? Por quê? / Por que não?

2 Match the pictures to the words. Then, complete the crossword puzzle.

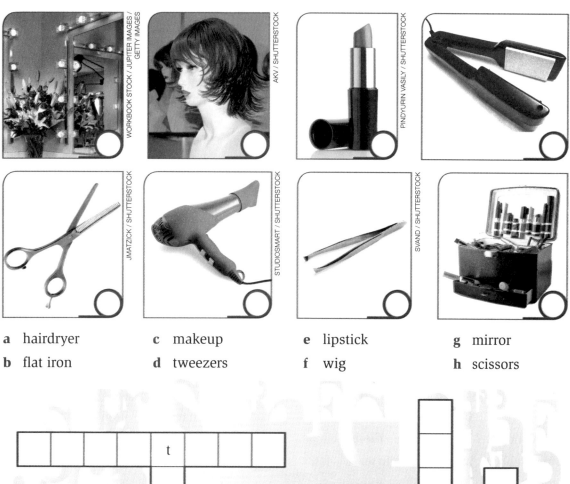

a hairdryer	**c** makeup	**e** lipstick	**g** mirror
b flat iron	**d** tweezers	**f** wig	**h** scissors

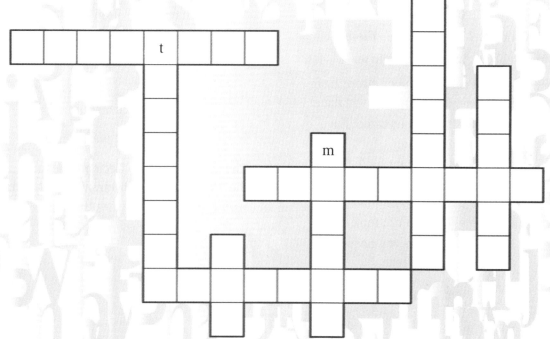

RAFAEL GENTILE

Additional Practice

For exercises 1 to 9, choose the best alternative.

1 A: The children's bedroom looks tidy.

B: It is! They _____.

a ( ) have just tidied it up

b ( ) haven't tidied it up yet

c ( ) did tidy it up

d ( ) tidied it up

e ( ) didn't tidy it up yet

2 Josh: _____ Japanese food?

Kevin: Yes, several times.

Josh: When _____ Japanese food for the first time?

Kevin: At a friend's party.

a ( ) Did you ever try; did you eat

b ( ) Did you ever try; have you eaten

c ( ) Have you ever tried; have you eaten

d ( ) Have you ever tried; did you eat

e ( ) Have you ever tried; have you eat

3 Nick: I _____ you for ages. Where _____?

Abby: I _____ back from New York.

Nick: Oh really? What _____ there?

Abby: I _____ an English course.

a ( ) haven't seen, have you been; have just come; have done; have taken

b ( ) didn't see, were you; came; have done; have taken

c ( ) haven't seen, did you be; have come; have done; took

d ( ) haven't seen, have you been; have just come; did you do; took

e ( ) haven't seen, have you been; did come; did do; did take

4 Jane: Mom, Sally _____ me to ask if I'll go to the movies with her. May I?

Mom: _____ your homework yet?

Jane: Well, I _____ homework for about 3 hours now, but I haven't finished it.

Mom: So you won't go. School comes first.

a ( ) have just called; Have you finished; has been doing

b ( ) have just called; Has finished; has been doing

c ( ) has just called; Has you finished; has been doing

d ( ) have just called; Have you finished; have been doing

e ( ) has just called; Have you finished; have been doing

5 A: How long have you been attending the Personal-Appearance Professional course?

B: _____.

a ( ) I have attended this course since last February

b ( ) I have been attending this course since last February

c ( ) I attended this course since last February

d ( ) I am attending this course since last February

e ( ) I attend this course since last February

6 The court has just decided the _____ of the three orphan children, but the children won't know the decision until next week.

a ( ) fate

b ( ) origin

c ( ) fear

d ( ) speech

e ( ) creed

7 The incredible story of Mrs. Thomas's survival from a shark attack has attracted _____ attention.

a ( ) any

b ( ) worldwide

c ( ) slaves

d ( ) social

e ( ) humanity

8 Calvin always has to watch every word he says to little Emma because she cries for no reason. She is extremely _____.

a ( ) strong

b ( ) rude

c ( ) polite

d ( ) sensitive

e ( ) brave

9 I was rude to my father _____ I was very upset. _____ I didn't mean to hurt him so bad.

a ( ) because, But

b ( ) so, And

c ( ) such as, Then

d ( ) when, Because

e ( ) in the end, So

10 Choose the alternative that best completes part of the lyrics of "I Hate You Then I Love You," sung by Celine Dion and Luciano Pavarotti.

I'd like to run away from you
_____ if I were to leave you I would die
I'd like to break the chains you put around me
_____ yet I'll never try
[…]

a ( ) But, And

b ( ) Then, Such as

c ( ) And, Afterwards

d ( ) When, Such as

e ( ) In the end, But

Refletindo sobre sua aprendizagem

Ao final desta unidade, você já é capaz de:

• Reconhecer citações, refletir sobre elas e associá-las a importantes momentos históricos e ao seu autor. ☐

• Identificar sinônimos de palavras pertencentes a um mesmo campo semântico. ☐

• Usar a língua portuguesa como mediadora na compreensão de um texto. ☐

• Estabelecer coesão e coerência de ideias usando alguns conectivos. ☐

• Reconhecer a diferença entre o emprego e a função comunicativa de verbos no *Simple Past* e no *Present Perfect*. ☐

• Produzir frases afirmativas, negativas e interrogativas no *Simple Past* e no *Present Perfect*. ☐

• Reconhecer o emprego e a função comunicativa de verbos no *Present Perfect Continuous*. ☐

• Associar imagem a um texto escrito. ☐

• Produzir frases interrogativas com *Present Perfect Continuous* e respondê-las usando os marcadores de tempo *for* e *since*. ☐

• Diferenciar palavras com sons similares. ☐

• Expressar sua opinião sobre alguns ícones da história. ☐

• Produzir uma carta formal com linguagem simples e coesa. ☐

Aprimorando sua aprendizagem

• Peça ajuda ao professor ou aos colegas para que esclareçam suas dúvidas.

• Refaça os exercícios.

• Visite a biblioteca da sua escola ou uma biblioteca pública e consulte livros de gramática e/ou faça leituras de seu interesse.

• Assista a filmes em inglês.

Further Practice 2
Units 3 & 4

1 Read the text and answer the questions in Portuguese.

The Surfaid Story

The Mentawai Islands are a chain of islands located in Indonesia. Nias Island is also in Indonesia.

In 1999, physician and surfer Dr. Dave Jenkins went on a surf charter to the Mentawai Islands with one goal in mind: to find perfect waves.

The surf proved to be everything he hoped for but he also found the Mentawai people, mostly women and children, suffering and dying from the ravages of malaria and other preventable diseases.

Dave found that he was unable to just walk away. It was a defining life moment. He sought support from long-time friend Dr. Steve Hathaway, an epidemiologist, and in January 2000 they co-founded SurfAid International, a non-profit organization dedicated to the alleviation of human suffering through community-based health programs.

In the aftermath of the 2004 Asian tsunami and 2005 Nias earthquake, SurfAid expanded its operations to Nias. With the support of the New Zealand and Australian governments, the global surfing and wider community, and most importantly the Mentawai and Nias people of the affected areas themselves, SurfAid has come to exemplify the healing power of cross-cultural partnerships.

Extracted from <http://www.surfaidinternational.org/about-us.html>.
Accessed on February 11, 2010.

a What was Dr. Dave Jenkins's main objective when he went to the Mentawai Islands?

_____

b What kind of problems did Dr. Dave Jenkins find on the Mentawai Islands?

_____

2 Find English words in the text for the following:

a médico _____

b danos _____

c procurou _____

d organização sem fins lucrativos _____

e terremoto _____

f poder de cura _____

3 Complete the sentences with the Present Perfect. Use the verbs in parentheses and the words given.

since	for	just	ever	never	already	yet	many times

a Mark _____ (be) in the same school _____ 2005.

He _____ (like) a school as much as he likes this particular one

now. He _____ (travel) abroad _____ with his

classmates and intends to go back to England as soon as he can, because he loved it there.

b I _____ (write) novels _____ about 10 years

now. The truth is I _____ (do) anything good enough to be published

_____, but I _____ (have) a new idea for a sci-fi

novel that will definitely be a hit.

c _____ (see) a UFO? Some people _____ (record)

videos that are said to show UFOs, but I don't believe they are real.

d My father and I _____ (swim) at a public pool

_____ three years. Unfortunately, my sister _____

(start) _____. She's too young.

e _____ (paint) a picture?

Not _____, but she _____ (attend) classes twice a

week.

f My classmates _____ (finish) their tests.

g _____ (be) on a musical contest? I _____ (sing) a

rock. It was amazing!

4 Complete the conversations with the Simple Past or the Present Perfect of the verbs in parentheses.

a **David:** _____ (hear) the news?

John: No. What happened?

David: Three days ago that man _____ (fall) from his apartment on the 6th floor!

b **Victor:** _____ (ever / break) a leg?

Tatiana: No, never.

Victor: _____ (break) my right leg and my left arm on my last vacation. Can you believe that?

Tatiana: What bad luck!

c **Larissa:** How many times _____ (see) *Superman Returns*?

Julie: Three times so far. The last time I _____ (rent) it on DVD was yesterday.

d **Manuel:** _____(ever / take) an English course abroad?

Pedro: No, but I _____ (speak) a lot of English when I visited Canada last summer.

5 Complete the sentences so that they mean the same as the original ones.

a I haven't seen this play before.

This is _____ this play.

b It's been a long time since I was last here.

I _____ a long time.

c We started waiting in this line half an hour ago.

We _____ half an hour.

d Susan called Pat at 6 o'clock. They are still talking on the phone. It's 8 now.

Susan _____ for 2 hours.

e Emil started reading the newspaper at eight. He is still reading it. It's nine now.

Emil _____.

6 Match the sentences with the best answers.

a It was their first meeting and Paul was determined to _____.

b We _____ with a number of German companies.

c Barbara _____ the good weather to paint the roof yesterday.

d I really don't know where the next party will _____.

e I no longer _____ for anything that happens in your life.

f There is a new Brazilian singer who has _____ in Europe.

g My mom is the one who _____ at home. My brother and I also help her.

( ) do business

( ) does the most chores

( ) make a good impression

( ) become successful

( ) take place

( ) take responsibility

( ) took advantage of

7 Use the linking words in the box to complete the sentences below.

| and   by the time   in the end   such as   beforehand |
| as soon as   in advance   afterwards   while   and |

a There are a great number of techniques that might help you to expand your vocabulary, _____ dividing the words into groups, forming new sentences with the words you have just learned, copying dictionary definitions, and many others.

b When you give a speech to a big audience, it's natural to feel nervous _____.

c I should warn you _____ that I'm not a very good singer.

d _____ you get home, log onto the net _____ download the video on globalization I asked you to watch.

e Unfortunately my car was stolen _____ I was on holiday.

f A couple of years _____ I bumped into her in the mall. She was very different from the old Katie I had met in the past.

g _____, my parents decided to go on a cruise to the Caribbean.

h The phone was ringing incessantly, but _____ she got in it had stopped.

PRE-READING

What kind of text is this? Who wrote this text?
What is it about?

Negro

(Langston Hughes)

I am a Negro:
Black as the night is black,
Black like the depths of my Africa.

I've been a slave:
Caesar told me to keep his door-steps clean.
I brushed the boots of Washington.

I've been a worker:
Under my hands the pyramids arose.
I made mortar for the Woolworth Building.

I've been a singer:
All the way from Africa to Georgia
I carried my sorrow songs.
I made ragtime.

I've been a victim:
The Belgians cut off my hands in the Congo.
They lynch me now in Texas.

I am a Negro:
Black as the night is black,
Black like the depths of my Africa.

Extracted from <http://www.pabook.libraries.psu.edu/palitmap/bios/Hughes__Langston.html>.
Accessed on December 6, 2009.

arose: surgiram
depths: profundezas
lynch: lincham
mortar: argamassa

ragtime: gênero musical afro-americano do séc. XIX
slave: escravo
sorrow: tristeza

After Reading

1 Match the verses of the poem to the pictures they represent.

a "I brushed the boots of Washington."

b "Black as the night is black."

c "The Belgians cut off my hands in the Congo."

d "I made mortar for the Woolworth Building."

e "I carried my sorrow songs."

Appendix 5

page 166

2 O eu lírico do poema *Negro* tem uma visão otimista ou pessimista da situação do povo africano ao longo da história? Por quê?

> **TIP**
>
> **Eu lírico** é a voz que fala no poema e nem sempre corresponde à do autor.

_____

_____

3 Leia o trecho abaixo, extraído de outro poema do mesmo autor. Compare o eu lírico deste poema com o eu lírico do poema da página 80.

I Dream a World

[...]

A world I dream where black or white,

Whatever race you be,

Will share the bounties of the earth

And every man is free

[...]

Extracted from <http://www.kansasheritage.org/crossingboundaries/idream.html>.
Accessed on December 12, 2009.

_____

_____

Vocabulary in Use

1 Brazilian society has been strongly influenced by African culture. Part of this influence is shown below. Read the sentences and match them to the photos they represent.

a It is a traditional African dish, made with lady's fingers (okra) and onions, shrimp, peppers, and oil.

b It is a religion based on African beliefs. It is also practiced in different countries, and it has as many as two million followers.

c It is a vibrant style of music that dates back hundreds of years and is rooted in Afro-Brazilian culture. It's music that goes straight to the soul!

d It is a martial art with over 400 hundred years of history. It is a style of self-defense that stands against weapons and firearms.

e It came from West Africa and Angola with the slave trading to Brazil in the 1600s. It is an African rhythm mixed with Brazilian music that has evolved into today's carnival.

maracatu

capoeira

samba

caruru

candomblé

Grammar in Use

PAST PERFECT

FORMAÇÃO: **HAD** + PARTICÍPIO PASSADO DO VERBO PRINCIPAL

Forma afirmativa	We **had read** the poem before we wrote the essay.
Forma negativa	We **hadn't read** the poem before we wrote the essay.
Forma interrogativa	**A: Had** you **read** the poem before you wrote the essay? **B:** Yes, we had. / No, we hadn't.
Formas abreviadas	**'d** = had **hadn't** = had not

USO

O **Past Perfect** é utilizado para indicar a ocorrência de uma ação no passado, antes de outra ação também no passado. Usamos o **Simple Past** para indicar a segunda ação ocorrida no passado.	When the ambulance arrived, the poor man had already died. <center>⇓ ⇓</center><center>(2nd action) (1st action)</center>The play hadn't started when I arrived at the theater. <center>⇓ ⇓</center><center>(1st action) (2nd action)</center>

O **Past Perfect** geralmente vem acompanhado de palavras como **when**, **after**, **before**, **already**, **yet**.

1 Match.

a When it started raining…

b By the time I turned on the TV…

c The teacher got disappointed…

d Why didn't you thank your parents…

e Did you get a ride…

( ) … after she found out we hadn't done our homework.

( ) … after you had missed the bus?

( ) … for all they had done for you?

( ) … the talk show had already finished.

( ) … I hadn't finished jogging yet.

2 Complete the sentences using the Past Perfect. The first one is done for you.

a The soccer match started at 9:00. I got to the stadium at 9:30.

When I got to the stadium, *the soccer match had already started*.

b Mark finished lunch at 1:00 p.m. I called him at 3:00 p.m.

When I called Mark, _____.

c The dancing contest was difficult for Monica. She didn't have enough training.

Because _____, the dancing contest was difficult.

d The detective found out who the burglar was. He left his fingerprints on the door handle.

The detective found out who the burglar was because _____

_____

e We finally got to the hospital. We drove around for hours.

After _____, we finally got to the hospital.

f I was 20 years old. I traveled abroad for the first time.

I _____ before I was 20 years old.

3 Answer the questions below according to the clues in parentheses. The first two alternatives are done for you.

a Were you in time to call Angela? (Yes)
Yes, I had already called Angela when you arrived.

b Were you in time to read the new contract? (No)
No, I hadn't time to read the new contract before you arrived.

c Were you in time to pay your school fees? (No)

_____

d Were you in time to cancel the hotel reservation? (Yes)

_____

e Were you in time to do the two jobs? (No)

_____

f Were you in time to meet the new teacher? (Yes)

_____

4 Ms. Miller's maid was very sick and spent 15 days away from work. She came back to work this morning and was shocked to see how messy Ms. Miller's house was. Compare the two pictures and decide what the maid had done by the end of the day. Ask questions using the cues given. Then answer the questions according to picture 2. The first one is done for you.

a organize the books on the shelves

   A: *Had the maid organized the books on the shelves?*

   B: *Yes, she had.*

b sweep the floor

_____

_____

c decorate the room with daisies

_____

_____

d take the coffee table out

_____

_____

e change the picture on the wall

_____

_____

f clean the sofa

_____

_____

Picture Dictionary 5

page 160

PAST PERFECT CONTINUOUS

FORMAÇÃO: **HAD BEEN** + VERBO PRINCIPAL + **ING**

Forma afirmativa	The singer **had been carrying** his sorrow songs all the way from Africa to Georgia.
Forma negativa	The singer **hadn't been carrying** his sorrow songs all the way from Africa to Georgia.
Forma interrogativa	**A: Had** the singer **been carrying** his sorrow songs all the way from Africa to Georgia? **B:** Yes, he had. / No, he hadn't.

USO

O **Past Perfect Continuous** é utilizado para expressar uma ação que estava acontecendo no passado antes de uma outra ação também no passado. Damos ênfase à ação que ocorreu primeiro entre ações no passado.	The children hadn't been waiting for a long time when their parents picked them up. How long had the players been exercising when the match started? They had been exercising for 15 minutes when the match started.

5 Read the text below about **Wangari Maathai**, a Kenyan writer and political activist. Underline the correct verb form.

Wangari Maathai, a Kenyan writer and political **activist**, is one of many female voices to fight for human rights in the African continent. Born in 1940, she **won / had won** the Nobel Peace Prize in 2004. By then the Green Belt Movement which she **founded / had founded** in 1977 was known worldwide and she **campaigned / had been campaigning** actively against deforestation. She **had even been arrested / has even been arrested** several times and **was suffering / had suffered** injuries when attacked while she **was planting / had planted** trees in a public space as part of a protest.

Based on <http://womenshistory.about.com/od/wangarimaathai/p/wangari_maathai.htm>; <http://nobelprize.org/nobel_prizes/peace/laureates/2004/maathai-bio.html>. Accessed on February 20, 2010.

6 Join the pairs of sentences. Use the words in parentheses and the Past Perfect Continuous. The first one is done for you.

a Mr. Thompson worked in the garden for an hour this morning. He took a rest.
(after) *After Mr. Thompson had been working in the garden for an hour this morning, he took a rest.*

b Maurren Maggi trained for years. She won a gold medal in the women's long jump at the Olympic Games in 2008.
(before) _____.
_____

c His tooth ached all night. He made an appointment to see the dentist the following morning.
(so) _____
_____

d They played soccer for hours yesterday. It suddenly began to rain.
(when) _____
_____

e We were very tired in the evening. We helped at the farm all day long.
(because) _____
_____

Reading

Tropical Multiculturalism

In the 1930s, the situation of blacks improved somewhat as immigration declined and ideological winds shifted. The 1930s were the era of the Afro-Brazilian Congresses in Recife (1934) and Bahia (1937) and of the Black Brazilian Conference (1940). It was in 1934 that Article 113 of the Brazilian Constitution declared that "All are equal before the law" and that "there will be no privileges or distinctions by reason of birth, sex, race, profession, country, social class, wealth, religious belief, or political ideas". It was also in the 1930s that Afro-Brazilians in São Paulo formed *A Frente Negra Brasileira* (The Black Brazilian Front) to protest precisely against the same discriminations based on race, wealth, and social class presumably prohibited by the Constitution, in a movement that mobilized thousands of blacks before it was banned by the populist dictator Vargas in 1938.

At the same time, anthropologist Gilberto Freyre, a student of the antiracist Franz Boas, formulated the theory of "racial democracy" in his 1933 *Casa Grande e Senzala* (literally, "Big House and the Slave Quarters" but translated as "The Masters and the Slaves"). Rather than see Afro-Brazilians as the cause of Brazil's "inferiority", Freyre emphasized the many-faceted contribution of blacks and Indians to Brazil's cultural mix. In the patriarchal system typical of Brazilian slavery, according to Freyre, African influences "carried" by black cooks and mammies allowed for a certain cultural democracy. Unlike other multiracial societies in the Americas, Brazilian social life was characterized by exceptional familiarity between the races.

[…]

Extracted from *Tropical Multiculturalism: A Comparative History of Race in Brazilian Cinema and Culture*. Robert Stam, author. Published by Duke University Press. Place of publication: Durhan, NC. Publication year: 1997. page 79.

before: perante
by reason of: por causa de
many-faceted: multifacetada
presumably: supostamente
rather than: em vez de

shifted: mudaram de direção
somewhat: um pouco
wealth: bens, posses
winds: ventos (sentido metafórico)

After Reading

1 Choose the word or expression that does not belong in each group. The first word on each line is from the text.

a	improved	got better	enriched	diminished
b	discrimination	equality	prejudice	racism
c	mobilized	brought together	interested	separated
d	banned	eliminated	encouraged	prohibited
e	allowed for	ended	gave room to	permitted
f	exceptional	extraordinary	not frequent	great

2 Choose the best alternative according to the text.

2.1 Which of these events are not related to the ideological changes in Brazilian society that started in the 1930s?

a ( ) The decline in the number of immigrants.

b ( ) The introduction of an antiracist article in the Constitution.

c ( ) The organization of conferences on themes related to the black community.

2.2 The Black Brazilian Front was created to protest against:

a ( ) the Constitution.

b ( ) all forms of discrimination.

c ( ) the dictator Vargas.

2.3 The central idea of Gilberto Freyre's *Casa Grande e Senzala* is that:

a ( ) Afro-Brazilians are the cause of Brazil's inferiority.

b ( ) Afro-Brazilians and Indians formed a separate democratic society in Brazil.

c ( ) Afro-Brazilians and Indians contributed to Brazil's cultural mix.

2.4 According to Freyre, the multiracial society in Brazil:

a ( ) had more interaction between descendents of European and African people.

b ( ) was very similar to other multiracial societies in the Americas.

c ( ) did not give room to a cultural mix in Brazil.

3 Read the poem below and answer the questions in Portuguese.

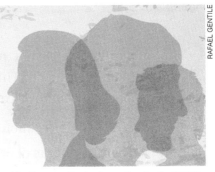

True Brotherhood

(Ella Wheeler Wilcox)

God, what a world, if men in street and mart
Felt that same kinship of the human heart
Which makes them, in the face of flame and flood,
Rise to the meaning of true Brotherhood!

Extracted from <http://www.readbookonline.net/readOnLine/21864>.
Accessed on January 31, 2010.

a Qual é a principal mensagem desse poema?

_____

_____

b No ponto de vista do eu lírico, onde se encontra a origem da fraternidade entre os homens?

_____

_____

c É possível estabelecer uma relação entre esse poema e o que se encontra na página 80? Mencione os principais pontos de aproximação.

_____

_____

4 Na unidade 1 do volume 1, verificamos que o poema organiza-se em versos que se agrupam em uma ou mais estrofes.

a Quantas estrofes e versos há no poema "True Brotherhood"?

_____

b Verificamos também que a rima das palavras é usada para representar uma das características do poema: a sonoridade. Que pares de palavras rimam entre si nesse poema?

_____

c A repetição de palavras é outro recurso usado em poemas para expressar sonoridade. Há palavras que se repetem no poema "True Brotherhood"?

_____

d A linguagem objetiva é aquela que oferece ao leitor informações precisas, transferindo a ele conhecimentos e fatos. É, portanto, uma visão imparcial do autor a respeito de algo. Já a linguagem subjetiva expressa a visão pessoal do autor, geralmente carregada de sentimentos e emoções. Qual das linguagens você reconhece nos poemas apresentados?

_____

e O destinatário de um poema é o público em geral. Em quais meios ele é geralmente veiculado?

_____

Language in Action

1 The public library in your neighborhood sometimes offers free cultural lectures to anyone who would like to attend. This week the lectures are about Africa. Listen to part of yesterday's lecture about Museum Africa. Then check the correct alternatives.

a (   ) There are few exhibits there.

b (   ) There are works of art based on some artists' impressions of the Anglo-Boer War.

c (   ) There are no geological specimens on display.

d (   ) One hour is enough for you to visit the museum.

e (   ) The museum was founded in 1994.

2 Sophia and Kevin are high school students who like History very much. This week Sophia went to the public library and attended a lecture about people who have influenced Brazilian culture. Kevin couldn't go because of a high fever. Read their dialogue. Then make new dialogues with a classmate. Use the cues given.

Kevin: How has Africa influenced Brazilian culture?

Sophia: It has influenced Brazilian food, dance, and music.

A	B
Spain	cattle farming in the South
Portugal	June festivals
Germany	wheat production
Italy	the habit of eating pizza
the Netherlands	architecture in the Northeast region, especially in Recife
Japan	new farming and fishing techniques in the South and Southeast regions

Writing

Brazilian culture is enriched by the diversity of its people. Read the extracts of articles below. In pairs, write a paragraph about the influences in the region you live in.
Use some of the information given to help you.

[…] In the Northeast, the Bahia region has heavy African influence whereas in the coastal areas the staples of the menus usually include seafood, shellfish, and tropical fruits. […]

Extracted from <http://www.braziltravelinformation.com/brazil_culture.htm>.
Accessed on February 16, 2010.

[…] The South – with a climate unsuited to either coffee or sugar – became the destination of many German and Italian immigrants who raised cattle and grew a variety of crops. […]

Extracted from <http://www.everyculture.com/Bo-Co/Brazil.html>.
Accessed on February 16, 2010.

[…] especially Germans and Japanese, established themselves in isolated rural communities. In many small towns and rural areas in the South and Southeast during the 1920s and 1930s, children were educated in German or Japanese, and Portuguese was rarely spoken. […]

Extracted from <http://www.everyculture.com/Bo-Co/Brazil.html>.
Accessed on February 16, 2010.

[…] Urban architecture in Brazil owes much to the legacy of Portuguese colonialism. Cities such as Ouro Preto and Rio de Janeiro grew in importance long before industrialization had brought the factory or the automobile to Brazil. These cities, which influenced patterns of urban construction throughout the country, were largely modeled on Portuguese cities. […]

Extracted from <http://www.everyculture.com/Bo-Co/Brazil.html>.
Accessed on February 16, 2010.

Consultando outras fontes

filme: *Mandela – A luta pela liberdade* (Alemanha, França, Bélgica, África do Sul, Itália, Inglaterra, Luxemburgo, 2007; direção: Billie August)

livros: *Um passeio pela África* (Nova Fronteira, 2006; autor: Alberto Costa e Silva)

Reinvenções da África na Bahia (Annablume, 2004; autora: Patrícia de Santana Pinho)

música: "Mama África" (Chico César)

Singer

Although there are different professions related to arts and entertainment, the most popular one is singing, especially among teenagers. If someone wants to be a singer, he or she should think about getting appropriate training beforehand.

Singers interpret songs written by themselves or by somebody else. In order to do this properly, they need to learn a lot about music, such as melody, harmony, genres, and styles. Mostly, singers need to improve the use of their voices so that they can perform a wider range of vocal styles.

The job market for a singer is diverse. Choirs, bands, chamber groups, recording agencies, radio and TV stations, the internet, theaters, movies, churches, pubs... the options are endless.

If you want to become a certified singer, you can take a technical course. It is 800 hours long and you can take it while you are in high school.

Based on
<http://online.onetcenter.org/link/summary/27-2042.01>;
<http://www.careerplanner.com/Job-Outlook/
Musicians-Singers-and-Related-Workers.cfm>.
Accessed on February 9, 2010.

although: embora

beforehand: antes, em primeiro lugar

chamber groups: grupos que fazem música de câmera (*show* musical do tipo documentário que leva a plateia para cozinhas, banheiros, praias, automóveis, etc. É considerada "música para os olhos".)

endless: inesgotáveis, intermináveis

entertainment: diversão, entretenimento

improve: aperfeiçoar

mostly: principalmente

range: gama, escala

Para mais informações, acesse:

<http://carreiras.empregos.com.br/comunidades/campus/profissoes/musicos.shtm>;

<http://www.guiadomusico.com.br/legislacao.html>;

<http://www.unicamp.br/unicamp/unicamp_hoje/ju/outubro2008/ju412_pag12.php>.

1 Você gostaria de ser cantor? Por quê? Por que não?

2 Read the definitions below and label the photos.

backing vocal: a singer who sings in harmony with the lead vocalist, other backing vocalists, or alone but not singing the lead.

headphones: a device with a part to cover each ear through which you can listen to music, radio broadcasts, etc., without other people hearing.

isolation booth: a soundproof booth located within a television studio, used to prevent the occupant, usually a contestant in a game show, from hearing certain parts of the show.

loudspeaker: a piece of equipment that changes electrical signals into sounds, especially used in public places so that large numbers of people can hear someone speaking or music playing.

mic stand: it provides the support for various sizes and shapes of microphones. It allows the performer (musician or spoken word) to free up their hands to play an instrument.

microphone: a piece of equipment that you speak into to make your voice louder, or to record your voice or other sounds.

mixer: a piece of equipment or computer software which is used to control the sound levels or picture quality of recording or film.

Extracted from
<http://www.statemaster.com/encyclopedia>;
<http://dictionary.cambridge.org>;
<http://dictionary.reference.com>;
<http://en.wikipedia.org/wiki/Microfone_stand>.

DAVID HOSKING / ALAMY / OTHER IMAGES

SMITH COLLECTION / ICONICA / GETTY IMAGES

Additional Practice

For exercises 1 to 8, choose the best alternative.

1 **Justin:** How was the movie yesterday?

Aaron: Well, when I arrived there, the movie _____.

a ( ) has already started
b ( ) have yet started
c ( ) had start
d ( ) had already started
e ( ) have start

2 **Kim:** Hi, Joey. Did you get your driver's license?

Joey: You won't believe it. By the time I _____ to the place, the instructor _____.

a ( ) had got, had already left
b ( ) have got, have already left
c ( ) got, left
d ( ) got, had already left
e ( ) had get, had already left

3 **Mr. White:** Although my students _____ on the project for about five weeks, their report _____ ready by the date I had specified.

a ( ) had been working, had been
b ( ) had been working, wasn't
c ( ) have been working, have been
d ( ) have been working, wasn't
e ( ) haven't worked, have been

4 **A:** Have you ever thought about what would have happened if the giant space rock _____ the Earth?

B: Wow, that's an interesting discussion!

a ( ) had missed
b ( ) has missed
c ( ) hasn't missed
d ( ) hadn't missed
e ( ) have missed

5 "During the 19th century, German immigrants in Brazil settled mostly in rural areas, named colony. These colonies _____ by the Brazilian government, and the lands were distributed between the immigrants. [...]"

Extracted from <http://www.dvhh.org/dta/brazil/1824-1969.htm>. Accessed on February 18, 2010.

a ( ) have been created
b ( ) has been created
c ( ) had created
d ( ) had been
e ( ) had been created

6 "[...] The second appearance of the ghost was on Sunday night. Not long after the family _____ to bed, they were suddenly frightened by a terrible crash in the hall. Rushing downstairs, they found that a large suit of old armor _____ from its usual place on the stone floor. [...]"

Extracted from WILDE, Oscar. *The Canterville Ghost and Other Stories*. London: Penguin Readers, Pearson Education Limited, 2000. page 8.

a ( ) have gone, have fallen
b ( ) had gone, had fallen
c ( ) has gone, had fallen
d ( ) had gone, has fallen
e ( ) have gone, has fallen

7 All the artists expressed their _____ at the news of the director's death.

a ( ) slaves
b ( ) inferiority
c ( ) mortar
d ( ) sorrow
e ( ) victim

8 That businessman has brought a _____ of experience to our company.

a ( ) winds

b ( ) wealth

c ( ) community

d ( ) depths

e ( ) job

9 Choose the correct sequence of events represented by the sentence below.

By the time Tom arrived, I had already finished cooking.

a ( ) Tom arrived then I cooked.

b ( ) Tom arrived while I was cooking.

c ( ) I was cooking while Tom arrived.

d ( ) I cooked at the same time Tom arrived.

e ( ) I cooked then Tom arrived.

10 Which sentence best expresses the following sequence of events?

First Sarah studied for two hours then she took the exam.

a ( ) Sarah has been studying for two hours when she took the exam.

b ( ) Sarah is studying for two hours and then she took the exam.

c ( ) Sarah has studied for two hours when she took the exam.

d ( ) Sarah studied for two hours when she took the exam.

e ( ) Sarah had been studying for two hours when she took the exam.

Refletindo sobre sua aprendizagem

Ao final desta unidade, você já é capaz de:

• Reconhecer características específicas de um poema, como por exemplo, sonoridade e tipo de linguagem. ☐

• Interpretar e comparar o eu lírico em diferentes poemas. ☐

• Associar fotos que representam diferentes aspectos da cultura africana às suas definições verbais escritas. ☐

• Reconhecer o emprego e a função comunicativa de verbos no *Past Perfect* e no *Past Perfect Continuous*. ☐

• Produzir frases afirmativas, negativas e interrogativas utilizando o *Past Perfect*. ☐

• Produzir frases afirmativas, negativas e interrogativas utilizando o *Past Perfect Continuous*. ☐

• Usar a linguagem oral para perguntar e informar sobre a influência da cultura africana no Brasil. ☐

• Produzir um texto sobre diversidade cultural na sua região. ☐

Aprimorando sua aprendizagem

• Peça ajuda ao professor ou aos colegas para que esclareçam suas dúvidas.

• Refaça os exercícios.

• Visite a biblioteca da sua escola ou uma biblioteca pública e consulte livros de gramática e/ou faça leituras de seu interesse.

• Assista a filmes em inglês.

It's Time to Laugh

PRE-READING

Do you know these characters? Where can we find these comic strips?

RAFAEL GENTILE

Essentials of a Good Comic Strip

[...]

- A good comic strip presents one main idea to the reader.
- The main idea is presented in an amusing, humorous, or funny manner.
- Thinking skills are much more important than drawing skills in creating a good comic.
- A good comic is always simple. Drawings should be uncluttered. Heavy, clean lines are better for the newspaper than many light lines.
- Sometimes comic strip characters talk with each other.
- Any words used in dialogue balloons should be simple and clearly written.
- Don't be too much of a perfectionist. If your comic is clever and communicates your message, you've done a good job!

[...]

Source: Pennsylvania Newspaper Publishers' Association NIE Committee
Extracted from <http://fredericksburg.com/nie/StarSearch/PDFS/ComicStripEssentials.doc>.
Accessed on December 8, 2009.

amusing: divertida	**realized:** percebi
awesome: incríveis	**skills:** habilidades
characters: personagens	**uncluttered:** organizados,
clever: inteligente	pouco decorados

After Reading

1 Read "Essentials of a Good Comic Strip" and choose the most appropriate answer.

1.1 What does a good comic strip present to the reader?

   a ( ) A main idea.

   b ( ) A good drawing.

   c ( ) A main character.

1.2 How is this presented?

   a ( ) With good characters.

   b ( ) In a complicated drawing style.

   c ( ) In an amusing, humorous, or funny way.

1.3 What skills are essential in creating a good comic strip?

   a ( ) Writing and drawing skills.

   b ( ) Drawing skills.

   c ( ) Thinking skills.

1.4 What kind of words should appear in the balloons?

   a ( ) Words that are simple.

   b ( ) Words that are simple and clearly written.

   c ( ) Words that are clearly written, but in a complex style.

1.5 How do we know if the comic strip is good?

   a ( ) If it is artistic and hides the message.

   b ( ) If it is clever and delivers the message.

   c ( ) If it is confusing but delivers the message.

2 Read the first comic strip on page 96 again and answer the following questions.

  a Does Jon look happy?

_____

  b Who is Jon talking to?

_____

  c What is he talking about?

_____

3 Now go back to the second comic strip and underline the correct alternative.

The young boy can't play basketball because **he doesn't know how to / the ball he is using is not appropriate for this kind of game.**

4 Compare the two comic strips and check yes or no.

	Yes	No
a Do they present a main idea to the reader?	( )	( )
b Are they funny?	( )	( )
c Do they contain difficult vocabulary?	( )	( )
d Are they clearly written?	( )	( )
e Do they deliver their message?	( )	( )

Vocabulary in Use

1 Go back to the texts on page 96. Find a synonym for each adjective below. Use the glossary if necessary.

a nice _____

b important _____

c entertaining _____

d ordinary _____

e tidy _____

f large _____

g smart _____

2 Choose the adjectives in the box that are related to the ones in the mind maps. Write each adjective in the corresponding mind map.

| comic   common   convenient   decent   easy   funny |
| high standard   hilarious   humorous   ordinary-looking   plain   talented |

good

amusing

simple

Reprodução proibida. Art.184 do Código Penal e Lei 9.610 de 19 de fevereiro de 1998.

RAFAEL GENTILE

3 Write three sentences. Use *good*, *simple*, and *amusing*.

_____

_____

_____

Grammar in Use

REFLEXIVE PRONOUNS

myself
yourself
himself
herself
itself
ourselves
yourselves
themselves

USO

Os **reflexive pronouns** são usados quando o sujeito faz e sofre a ação do verbo; ou seja, sujeito e objeto do verbo são a mesma pessoa. Neste caso, o **reflexive pronoun** é posicionado após o verbo e concorda com o sujeito.	**The wife** couldn't control **herself** and ended up arguing with her husband in public.
Quando queremos dar ênfase ao sujeito ou ao objeto, o **reflexive pronoun** é posicionado logo após o sujeito ou no fim da oração.	**The students themselves** talked to the principal. (ênfase no sujeito) **The students** talked to the principal **themselves**. (ênfase no sujeito) The students talked to **the principal himself**. (ênfase no objeto)
Quando queremos dar a ideia de "sozinho" ou "sem ajuda", o **reflexive pronoun** é precedido de *by*.	Jack was sitting **by himself** in the corner of the café.

Notas

É possível usar o **reflexive pronoun** também após a construção *adjetivo + preposição*.	I'm **proud of myself** for winning the competition.
Alguns verbos como *wash*, *dress* e *shave*, não têm a sua forma reflexiva em inglês.	Does your father **shave** every day?
Entretanto, a forma reflexiva pode ser utilizada se for necessário deixar claro quem fez a ação.	My son is seven years old, so he can **dress himself** now. There are five people in my family. My mom **herself washes** all the family's clothes.

1 Circle the reflexive pronouns in the comic strips below.

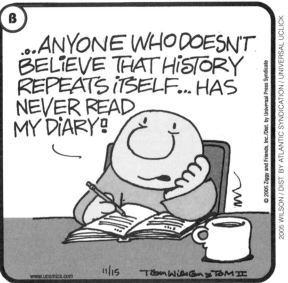

...beautifying yourself for him.

2 Read the extracts of the lyrics below. Fill in the gaps with the appropriate reflexive pronouns.

Ego
(Beyoncé)

[...]

It's on baby, let's get lost

You don't need to call into work 'cause you're the boss

For real, want you to show me how you feel

I consider _____ lucky, that's a big deal

[...]

Extracted from <http://www.elyrics.net/read/b/beyonce-lyrics/ego-lyrics.html>.
Accessed on February 3, 2010.

Naturally
(Selena Gomez)

How you choose to express _____

It's all your own and I can tell

It comes naturally, it comes naturally

[...]

Extracted from <http://www.elyrics.net/read/s/selena-gomez-lyrics/naturally-lyrics.html>.
Accessed on February 3, 2010.

Pretend That You're Alone
(Keane)

[...]

And love is just our way of looking out for _____

When we don't want to live alone

So step into the vacuum

Tear off your clothes and be born again

[...]

Extracted from <http://www.metrolyrics.com/pretend-that-youre-alone-lyrics-keane.html>.
Accessed on February 3, 2010.

TAG QUESTIONS

FORMAÇÃO: VERBO AUXILIAR/MODAL + PRONOME

Declaração afirmativa – *tag question* negativa	The meeting is on Saturday, **isn't it**?
Declaração negativa – *tag question* afirmativa	You just don't understand, **do you**?

USO

Tag questions são pedidos de confirmação do que foi dito anteriormente em forma de perguntas.	
Casos especiais	I am right, **am I not/aren't I**? Let's go, **shall we**? Don't come back here, **will you**? She may call, **may she not**? There were no mistakes, **were there**? Everybody has a PC, **don't they**?

3 Match.

a She cut herself yesterday,   (   ) have they?

b They haven't been satisfied,   (   ) aren't I?

c It is worth visiting Cuba,   (   ) doesn't she?

d Betty cooks her own meals,   (   ) mustn't you?

e You must apologize to her,   (   ) didn't she?

f Call me Siena,   (   ) will you?

g I am helping to collect the donations,   (   ) isn't it?

4 Read the comic strip. Then write a sentence to finish the story. Use a tag question.

5 Rewrite the proverbs using tag questions. The first one is done for you.

a Absence makes the heart grow fonder.
Absence makes the heart grow fonder, doesn't it?

b Actions speak louder than words.

_____

c There is no accounting for tastes.

_____

d Appearances are deceptive.

_____

e Ask no questions and hear no lies.

_____

f All is fair in love and war.

_____

g Those who live in glass houses shouldn't throw stones.

_____

h Curiosity killed the cat.

_____

i You cannot make an omelet without breaking eggs.

_____

6 Today is Celina's first day at work. She is a little bit confused, but her best friend Diana is helping her. Use question tags to complete their dialogue.

Diana: Celina, you know you have to arrive at work at 7:30, _____?

Celina: Yes, dear. But today there was a traffic jam and I called to tell you I was going to be late. You got my message, _____?

Diana: Yes, I did. Now, let's get to work, _____?

Celina: I'm not supposed to answer my cell phone here, _____?

Diana: You can answer your personal cell phone, but you can't talk for long. You couldn't do that at the place you worked before, _____?

Celina: No. You'll warn me if I do something wrong, _____?

Diana: Of course. I'm here for you.

Celina: OK. Your assistant is also going to help me, _____?

Diana: Yes, but remember: don't miss this opportunity, _____?

Reading

Chris Browne

Chris Browne was born in South Orange, N. J., in 1952 and grew up in suburban Wilton, Connecticut. The son of award-winning cartoonist Dik Browne, he assisted his father on the comic strips *Hi and Lois* and *Hagar the Horrible*. He contributed gag writing to Hagar from its inception in 1972.

With his father, Chris co-authored *Hagar the Horrible's Very Nearly Complete Viking Handbook* in 1985. When Dik Browne retired in 1988, Chris continued to write and draw the strip.

Hagar now appears in more than 1,900 newspapers around the world. It is translated into 13 languages and appears in 45 countries. The little red-bearded Viking has also appeared in advertisements for IBM, Mug Root Beer, Skol Ale, and in the opening title of the *Caroline in the City* NBC television show. Hagar has appeared in his own CBS special and as a feature of the new Universal theme park Islands of Adventure: Toon Lagoon.

[...]

Extracted from <http://www.cartoonistgroup.com/properties/template_about.php?id=185>.
Accessed on December 15, 2009.

Hagar

He may look like a fierce warrior, but once you get past the sword and shield, Hagar's a loving husband, a devoted father and family man, and a reluctant taxpayer. And while he has a voracious appetite for pillaging and plundering, they pale in comparison to his appetite for Helga's home-cooked meals.

Helga

Hagar's demanding wife. Dressed always in her horned helmet, she is a true Valkyrie, besting the beleaguered Hagar in battles on the home front. [...] Helga is a devoted wife and mother, often doing what's best for her family whether they want it or not.

Extracted from <http://www.kingfeatures.com/features/comics/hagar/charactMaina.htm>.
Accessed on December 15, 2009.

advertisements: propagandas
award-winning: premiado
battles: batalhas
beleaguered: cercado (por um inimigo)
besting: superando
co-authored: criou em conjunto
demanding: exigente
devoted: dedicada

fierce: feroz
gag: histórias de humor
horned helmet: capacete com chifre
inception: começo de uma instituição
pale: perdem a importância
pillaging and plundering: saquear
red-bearded: com barba ruiva
retired: aposentou-se

shield: escudo
sword: espada
taxpayer: contribuinte de impostos
Valkyrie: Valquíria (cada uma das divindades escandinavas que personificavam as virtudes dos heróis e que serviam uma mistura de água e mel ou cerveja aos que morriam em combate)

After Reading

1 Read the text on page 104 and write T (true), F (false), or DK (don't know).

a (   ) Chris Browne's father has received a prize.

b (   ) In 1988, Chris continued to write and draw *Hagar the Horrible* because his father died.

c (   ) *Hagar the Horrible* will become a fiction novel.

d (   ) The reader's first impression of Hagar might be wrong.

e (   ) Helga cares about her family.

2 The texts describing Hagar and Helga contain adjectives that refer to their personality. Take a look below.

Hagar is...
a fierce warrior a loving husband a devoted father a reluctant taxpayer

Helga is...
a demanding wife a true Valkyrie a devoted wife and mother

Now complete the following sentences using the adjectives given. Use the glossary if necessary.

determined   generous   open-minded   honest   ambitious   sociable

a Grandpa is a _____ man. He loves being with other people.

b Little Tommy is an _____ boy. He won't lie to Ms. Robinson about his late homework.

c If you are _____, you can learn a new language much faster.

d No doubt Philip will become a successful manager one day. He is very _____.

e It is simply great to get presents from Aunt Ethel. She is the most _____ person in our family.

f My parents always try to understand me when I'm in deep trouble. They are _____.

3 Answer the following questions in Portuguese.

a A partir dos elementos essenciais que as tirinhas devem apresentar, descritos na página 96, qual das tirinhas lidas melhor corresponde a tais exigências? Justifique a sua escolha.

_____

_____

b Qual das tirinhas provoca maior reflexão no leitor?

_____

_____

Language in Action

1 Mauricio de Sousa, the creator of *Monica's Gang*, is recognized as one of the best cartoonists (11) in the world. Listen to part of his story and fill in the gaps with the correct words.

From the drawing board of Brazilian cartoonist,

_____, and filmmaker Mauricio de Sousa, over 200

cartoon _____ for kids have come to life, led by the signature

group, *Monica's Gang*. Mauricio, founder and CEO of Mauricio de Sousa Productions, the

fourth-largest _____ in the world, leads a team of over 150 artists [...]

Born in Santa Isabel, a small town outside of São Paulo, the son of parents who were both

artists, Mauricio loved to _____ and draw from early on. As a young man, he

moved to the big city and started out in _____ as a police reporter for the

Folha de São Paulo newspaper. But his dream was to _____ comics. In 1959,

the newspaper ran his first _____, starring a little blue pup named Blu.

It marked the starting point for a highly successful international career that

continues to expand in Brazil and around the globe.

[...]

Extracted from <http://www.turmadamonica.com.br/ingles/mauricio/autor.htm>.
Accessed on February 18, 2010.

2 Read the dialogue below. Then talk to a classmate about the personality of some **characters** (12) created by Mauricio de Sousa. Use the adjectives given.

A: What do you think of Monica?

B: In my opinion, she's intelligent, bright, and strong. On the other hand, she's usually angry and sometimes abrupt.

Monica – She's the gang's leader.
Maggy – She's Monica's best friend.
Jimmy Five – He has difficulty pronouncing *r* sounds. He loves sports, music, and the outdoors.
Smudge – He's Jimmy's best friend. He doesn't like water.

POSITIVE ADJECTIVES		
adorable	bright	cooperative
courageous	energetic	fabulous
friendly	funny	helpful
hilarious	intelligent	persistent
spirited	strong	trustworthy

NEGATIVE ADJECTIVES		
abrupt	afraid	angry
awful	boring	cowardly
dangerous	jealous	nervous
silly	timid	weak
frightened		

Writing

Chuck Billy is also a famous character created by Mauricio de Sousa. This character doesn't like to get up early. He really likes going fishing and sitting under a tree.

MAURICIO DE SOUSA PRODUÇÕES LTDA

- Now go back to page 96. Read the characteristics of comic strips again.
- Work in pairs to create your own comic strip.
- Choose a topic that is important to both of you.
- Think of the characters. Draw them.
- Write their dialogue in bubbles.
- Exchange comic strips with other classmates so that everybody can see each other's comic strips.

Picture Dictionary 6

page 161

Consultando outras fontes

filme: *Dear Mr. Watterson* (EUA, 2001; diretor: Joel Allen Schroeder)   **site:** <http://www.dearmrwatterson.com>

livro: *Mauricio de Sousa – Biografia em Quadrinhos* (Panini, 2007; autor: Mauricio de Sousa)

In the Job Market

Prepress Technician

Have you ever wondered who, besides the author, is behind the process of making your favorite comic book? Well, if you have, you'll now be introduced to one of the professionals who make sure you get your hands on a new comic strip or book every week. Meet the prepress technician.

This is the professional who plans out and develops graphic projects for publicity through the prepress production process, using aesthetic criteria. He or she composes layouts of digital files, illustrations and graphics – using specific computer software. In order to maintain quality standards, this individual also controls the color reproduction process and creates digital and analogue proofs to improve images so that mistakes can be corrected before copies are printed and reach people's hands. In short, a prepress technician produces material for print reproduction.

As a prepress technician, you will work for graphic companies or organizations; graphic services bureaus; equipment and production goods suppliers; ad agencies; or publishing houses.

Those wanting to become prepress technicians must take a 1200-hour course (approximately two years).

Based on <http://my.monster.com/job-profiles/Prepress-Technician.aspx?keyword=graphic technician&re=1000>;
<http://www.wisegeek.com/how-do-i-become-a-prepress-technician.htm>;
<http://www.careerplanner.com/Job-Outlook/Prepress-Technicians-and-Workers.cfm>;
<http://online.onetcenter.org/link/summary/51-5022.00>.
Accessed on February 5, 2010.

ad agencies (advertising agencies): agências de publicidade

aesthetic criteria: critérios estéticos

besides: além do

carry out: realizam

graphic services bureaus: empresas que fornecem serviços gráficos

in short: em poucas palavras

plan out: planejam cuidadosa e detalhadamente

production goods: insumos

suppliers: fornecedores

Para mais informações, acesse:

<http://catalogonct.mec.gov.br/et_producao_industrial/t_pre_impressao_grafica.php>;

<http://www.senai.br/br/Almanaque/snai_vc_alm_pch_det.aspx?idPro=227>.

1 Você gostaria de ser técnico em pré-impressão gráfica? Por quê? / Por que não?

2 Write the words in the box in the correct places.

| bubble | caption | cover | headline | lead | sound effect |

Google Stands Firm Amid Complaints in Europe

By JAMES KANTER

BRUSSELS — Facing a new wave of antitrust complaints in Europe, Google stood firm on Wednesday, saying it would not offer concessions to companies that have accused it of abusing its market power in online searches and advertising.

Google said it was preparing a response to questions sent by European antitrust regulators after it faced accusations from companies, including a unit of its archrival, Microsoft. "We haven't done anything wrong," said Julia Holtz, the senior competition counsel for Google. As a result, she said, the company did not consider it necessary to offer "any sort of commitment" in response to the complaints.

The complaints to the European Commission indicate rising frustration among competitors with Google's strength in the online advertising business and with its business practices.

In some European countries, Google has more than 80 percent of the market for Internet searches and advertising linked to them. European Commission officials have said in the past, however, that market dominance was not, in and of itself, sufficient cause for antitrust sanctions.

Antitrust experts said that Google's decision to publicize the complaints itself showed the company's determination to try to stop the case before it advanced any further. "This is the time for Google's lawyers to be highly proactive, and to go with their knives sharpened and daggers in their mouths to try and kill the investigation," said Dennis Oswell, an antitrust lawyer at Oswell & Vahida in Brussels.

The commission confirmed that it had received three complaints against Google and said it was examining them.

Extracted from *The New York Times*, February 25, 2010.

Follow your dreams...

Billy Elliot

Additional Practice

For exercises 1 to 9, choose the best alternative.

1 A: I've heard Sarah is taking that course again.

B: Yeah. She has decided to give _____ a second chance.

a ( ) myself
b ( ) yourself
c ( ) ourselves
d ( ) herself
e ( ) himself

2 A: In order to make him express _____ properly, you must give him some time.

B: Absolutely.

a ( ) myself
b ( ) herself
c ( ) themselves
d ( ) ourselves
e ( ) himself

3 Joshua and his girlfriend Claire are proud of _____ because they succeeded in the finals.

a ( ) myself
b ( ) yourself
c ( ) ourselves
d ( ) themselves
e ( ) himself

4 A: You don't know where Ann is, _____?

B: I'm afraid she has already left.

a ( ) do you
b ( ) does she
c ( ) is she
d ( ) are you
e ( ) don't you

5 Gabriella: Come on, Brian. Lia would help you if you asked her to, _____?

Brian: I guess so.

a ( ) isn't she
b ( ) would she
c ( ) wouldn't you
d ( ) wouldn't she
e ( ) would she

6 Janice: You called the maid, _____?

Ethan: You know I called her. You were there, _____?

a ( ) do you; were you
b ( ) didn't you; weren't you
c ( ) did you; were you
d ( ) didn't you; were you
e ( ) you didn't; you were

7 I think Mike is too _____. He always asks his employees to redo their work as if nothing were done correctly.

a ( ) true
b ( ) ordinary
c ( ) funny
d ( ) comic
e ( ) demanding

8 Damian wears T-shirts, old jeans, and sneakers. He is too _____. I told him to buy some _____ clothes if he wants to work as the CEO's assistant at that company.

a ( ) tidy, common
b ( ) smart, cheap
c ( ) clever, good
d ( ) nice, uncluttered
e ( ) ordinary-looking, decent

9 A: Have you read the book *Don Quixote de La Mancha*?

B: Sure. It is about a man that believes he is a true knight with a _____ and a _____ fighting against imaginary enemies.

a ( ) flower, gun

b ( ) book, sword

c ( ) lance, shield

d ( ) award, battle

e ( ) character, skill

10 Choose the alternative that presents the best synonyms for the words in bold.

Professor Stevens is extremely **smart** when it comes to making money, but he is not a **nice** person when it comes to respecting others.

a ( ) tidy, main

b ( ) amusing, heavy

c ( ) clever, good

d ( ) important, uncluttered

e ( ) decent, hilarious

Refletindo sobre sua aprendizagem

Ao final desta unidade, você já é capaz de:

• Reconhecer as principais características do gênero cartum. ☐
• Estabelecer comparação entre dois cartuns. ☐
• Identificar sinônimos de adjetivos. ☐
• Relacionar palavras pertencentes a um mesmo campo semântico. ☐
• Reconhecer o emprego e a função comunicativa dos pronomes reflexivos em diferentes contextos. ☐
• Formar *tag questions* e utilizá-las adequadamente em variadas situações comunicativas. ☐
• Selecionar adjetivos apropriados para descrever diferentes personalidades. ☐
• Utilizar a linguagem oral para expressar opinião pessoal sobre alguns personagens de histórias em quadrinhos. ☐
• Produzir uma tirinha a partir dos conhecimentos adquiridos. ☐

Aprimorando sua aprendizagem

• Peça ajuda ao professor ou aos colegas para que esclareçam suas dúvidas.
• Refaça os exercícios.
• Visite a biblioteca da sua escola ou uma biblioteca pública e consulte livros de gramática e/ou faça leituras de seu interesse.
• Assista a filmes em inglês.

1 Silvia is a Brazilian woman who has graduated in gastronomy. She has been to Hertfordshire, England, to take an award-winning cooking course. She spent three weeks there. By the time she came back, she had learned and done different things. Find out what by completing the sentences below. Use the verbs in the box in the Past Perfect.

cross	eat	master	meet	spend

Silvia…

a _____ different dishes and culinary techniques.

b _____ people from different parts of the world.

c _____ the English Channel.

d _____ in famous restaurants.

e _____ much money on short tours.

2 Read the small texts. Then complete the sentences. Use the Past Perfect Continuous.

a My friends and I played volleyball yesterday. An hour after we started playing, it began raining.

My friends and I _____

_____ when it began raining.

b We went to see a play on Saturday. The actors began performing. After about half an hour the lights went out.

The actors _____

_____ when the lights went out.

c Peter got a temporary job in a shop near his house. Two months later the shop closed down.

At the time the shop closed down, Peter _____

_____ .

d I set up an appointment with Dr. Curtis. I arrived at his office and waited for him. After forty-five minutes, his secretary told me he wouldn't come in time.

By the time Dr. Curtis's secretary told me he wouldn't come in time, I _____ _____.

3 Some verbs in the sentences below are wrong. Underline and correct them.

a Susan left the university before she had taken all her final exams. _____

b Peter had been working on his new project for over two hours when the computer had broken. _____

c The euphoric fans had been waiting in line for six hours. _____

d By the time of the trial, Jackson had been being in jail for about six months. _____

e I didn't know who that girl was. I had never seen her before. _____

f At last the train came. I had waited for an hour. _____

g I was very hungry when I arrived home. I had worked hard all day long. _____

4 Check the appropriate alternative to complete the answers.

4.1 A: Who went to the party with you?

B: I went _____.

   a ( ) by myself   **b** ( ) by yourself   **c** ( ) by himself

4.2 A: Did Dylan ask for help to carry all those boxes?

B: No, he did it _____.

   a ( ) themselves   **b** ( ) himself   **c** ( ) ourselves

4.3 A: How are the athletes feeling after this exhausting marathon?

B: They're tired, but they're proud of _____.

   a ( ) themselves   **b** ( ) myself   **c** ( ) herself

5 Complete the following sentences. Use the verbs in the box and the reflexive pronouns. Make the necessary changes.

cut   lock   hurt   burn   teach   blame   talk to

a Be careful! That chicken soup is very hot. Don't _____.

b I'm trying to _____ Chinese, but I don't think it is working.

c It isn't Mary's fault. She doesn't have to _____.

d Carlos spends most of his time alone, so it's not surprising that he _____
_____.

e Xavier _____ while he was shaving.

f The Smiths couldn't get back into the house. They had _____
outside.

g My cousin John was lucky when he fell down the stairs. He didn't _____
_____ very seriously.

6 Match.

a Percy told you he would always love you,

b Steve does his homework before watching TV every morning,

c There is nobody in front of our house,

d The students had already solved all the Math exercises,

e I am the one who has given you a shoulder to cry on,

f Bring me that book,

(   ) is there?

(   ) hadn't they?

(   ) didn't he?

(   ) will you?

(   ) aren't I?

(   ) doesn't he?

7 Complete the text. Use *as* or *like*.

_____ all of you know, I'm Francis Curtis, CEO of this company. Before

reaching this position, I'd already worked _____ a cartoonist in a local

newspaper. Nowadays, people look up to me. They treat me _____ a pop

star, _____ someone who really deserves to be treated well. I love lots of

things in the business world, _____ traveling abroad to do business with

foreigners or bargain with a customer. People say I work _____ a slave, but

_____ this is my job, nothing can be done. I really don't know what to do to

have fun _____ my partners do. This is something I still have to learn.

8 Read the cartoon and answer the questions in Portuguese.

a Who is the main character?

_____.

b A pergunta da personagem ao espelho faz referência a outra história. Que história é essa?

Quem faz esta mesma pergunta na história?

_____

_____.

c A que provérbio popular a última fala se refere?

_____

7 Water and Sanitation for All!

PRE-READING

The following article is an excerpt from a magazine. Read the title. What kind of information do you think you will find?

Targeting Sanitation

CEES VAN DE GUCHTE and VEERLE VANDEWEERD address the environmental aspects and costs of meeting the World Summit on Sustainable Development target on improved sanitation, and describe the growing global consensus on alternative low-cost technologies.

Some four children die every minute in developing countries from diseases caused by unsafe water and inadequate sanitation. On average, 250 million cases of gastroenteritis occur worldwide every year from bathing in contaminated water, and 50,000-100,000 people die from infectious hepatitis. The global burden of human disease caused by sewage pollution of coastal waters has been estimated at 4 million lost person-years annually.

The deterioration of the aquatic environment is visible around the globe. The discharge of untreated domestic wastewater has been identified as a major source of pollution in most of the UNEP Regional Seas. Untreated sewage affects over 70 per cent of coral reefs, precious habitats are disappearing and biodiversity is decreasing, fishing and agricultural potential are being lost, while poor water quality is reducing income from tourism and the value of real estate.

Such concerns have helped push the international community to ensure that the targets of the 2000 Millennium Development Goals and the 2002 World Summit on Sustainable Development (WSSD) address improved access to safe drinking water and adequate sanitation.

The WSSD agreed target on water and sanitation is "To halve, by the year 2015, the proportion of people who are unable to reach or to afford safe drinking water and the proportion of people who do not have access to basic sanitation".

Extracted from *Our Planet: The Magazine of The United Nations Environment Programme*, v. 14, n. 4, p. 19.

---

afford: arcar com os custos de
burden: carga, peso
concerns: preocupações
discharge: descarga (emissão)
ensure: garantir

halve: reduzir pela metade
improved: melhorado
income: renda
sewage: esgoto
target: objetivo

UNEP (United Nations Environment Programme): Programa Ambiental das Nações Unidas
wastewater: água residual
WSSD (World Summit on Sustainable Development): Conferência Mundial de Desenvolvimento Sustentável

After Reading

1 Complete the sentences according to the text on page 116.

   a _____ and _____ kill four children a minute in developing countries.

   b Untreated sewage causes the disappearance of _____, the decrease of _____, as well as the loss of _____ _____.

2 Label the five oceans in the map below.

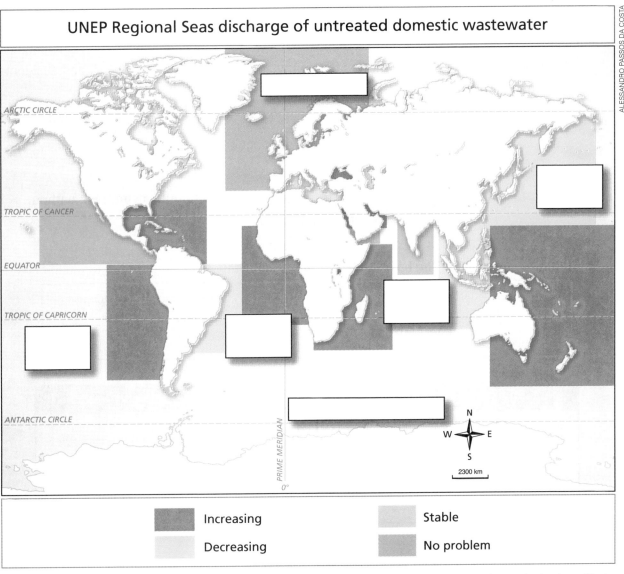

UNEP Regional Seas discharge of untreated domestic wastewater

ARCTIC CIRCLE

TROPIC OF CANCER

EQUATOR

TROPIC OF CAPRICORN

ANTARCTIC CIRCLE

PRIME MERIDIAN

0°

2300 km

- Increasing
- Decreasing
- Stable
- No problem

ALESSANDRO PASSOS DA COSTA

Extracted from <http://www.unep.org/OurPlanet/imgversn/144/vandeweerd.html>.
Accessed on December 10, 2009.

Vocabulary in Use

1 Fill in the chart according to the information in the tip. Then translate the new words. The first one is done for you.

safe	unsafe	perigoso
treated		
polluted		
protected		
drinkable		
harmed		

2 Complete the sentences with the words formed in exercise 1.

a The machinery in that company was frequently _____, and accidents happened all the time.

b A great number of people still have access only to _____ water.

c _____ sewage causes the loss of about 4 million person-years annually.

d Fortunately the children were _____ during the fire.

e At that time, the river was _____ and children could swim there without coming into contact with toxic waste from local factories.

3 Write the expressions in the box in the appropriate column.

car pool   destruction of habitats   electric cars   greenhouse effect increase
preserve biodiversity   public transport   reduce CH4 emissions
reduce the number of trees that are cut down   renewable energy   traffic jam

Environmental problems	Environmental solutions

Grammar in Use

SOME, ANY, NO

Some e **any** podem ter a função de adjetivos (quando acompanham o substantivo) ou de pronome (quando substituem o substantivo).	**Some** four children die every minute in developing countries from diseases caused by unsafe water. **A:** Do you have **any** money with you? **B:** Yes, I have **some**. / No, I don't have **any**.

USO

Some (algum, alguns, alguma, algumas, um pouco de) Em frases afirmativas ou interrogativas que indiquem ofertas, sugestão ou convite, ou quando se aguarda uma resposta afirmativa.	We need to buy some sodas for the party. Would you like some coffee? Do you mind if I put on some music here?
Any (algum, alguns, algumas, nenhum, nenhuma) Em frases negativas e interrogativas.	I don't know any famous actors. Do you have any questions?

Notas

Any também é utilizado em sentenças afirmativas.	
a) Se o sentido for "qualquer".	Alternative low-cost technologies will be a global standard at any moment.
b) Se estiver precedido de uma condição com **if** (se).	**If** you have any environmental concerns, don't discharge untreated domestic wastewater.
c) Se estiver acompanhando palavras de sentido negativo como **never**, **rarely**, **seldom**, **hardly ever**, **without**, etc.	Some countries **rarely** have any good sanitation conditions.
No/None (nenhum, nenhuma) Em negações, sem haver outra palavra negativa na sentença.	They have **no** solution for the problem. We have **none** either.

1 List the food items below in the correct column. Consider (**+**) for the items Barbara has just bought at the supermarket and (**–**) for the items she hasn't bought.

(**+**) apples

(**+**) avocado

(**+**) bananas

(**+**) bread

(**+**) butter

(**–**) carrots

(**–**) cereal

(**–**) chicken

(**–**) corn

(**–**) crackers

(**+**) fish

(**–**) ice cream

(**–**) nuts

(**–**) peaches

(**+**) rice

(**+**) yogurt

Some	Any
bananas	

2 Underline the best word to complete each sentence below.

a The bird hasn't drunk **any / some** water today.

b Did you watch **no / any** films last month?

c I have **some / any** news for you.

d Steven is going to answer **no / any** e-mails tomorrow.

e There is **no / any** reason to worry about Dan.

f He has received many gifts, but his wife has received **no / none**.

g Would you care for **any / some** finger food?

h Bring **some / any** recyclable material next class.

i If you have **any / no** suggestions, contact me.

j We seldom eat **no / any** fattening food.

3 Match.

a I could finish my homework…

b Do you speak…

c She never…

d They don't have…

e I've had…

f Would you like…

g Have…

h Sorry, I have…

i None…

(   ) some more soup.

(   ) without any help.

(   ) some coffee?

(   ) of this luggage is mine.

(   ) any children.

(   ) no time now.

(   ) any other languages?

(   ) no difficulty understanding her.

(   ) does any work in the house.

4 Put the words in parentheses in the correct order to make sentences.

a **A:** How about going to the mall this evening?

B: Why? _____

(any / There / today / open / aren't / shops)

b **A:** What would you like to eat?

B: _____

(eggs / you / me / give / Could / please / some – int.)

c **A:** Let's go and eat in that fancy restaurant.

B: Wait! _____

(have / no / We / us / with / brought / money)

d **A:** Can you say that again?

B: _____

(is / this / ours / None of / money)

> O uso de **some, any** e **no** é válido para o emprego de seus compostos.

somebody / someone anybody / anyone nobody / no one
something anything nothing
somewhere anywhere nowhere

5 Choose the best word to complete each sentence below.

5.1 My husband thinks _____ is more devoted to my kids than I am.

   a ( ) somebody

   b ( ) nobody

   c ( ) somewhere

5.2 Louis couldn't find _____ DVDs in his locker. In my opinion, they might be _____ else in his office.

   a ( ) no, somewhere

   b ( ) any, anything

   c ( ) any, somewhere

5.3 Can _____ go wrong while I'm gone?

   a ( ) anything

   b ( ) anywhere

   c ( ) something

5.4 The coach didn't imagine _____ would play as well as Bart.

   a ( ) nobody

   b ( ) anyone

   c ( ) anything

5.5 You've traveled the whole world! Is there _____ you haven't been yet?

   a ( ) somewhere

   b ( ) nowhere

   c ( ) anywhere

5.6 If they find _____ to buy their tickets, they'll make _____ money.

   a ( ) anyone, any

   b ( ) someone, some

   c ( ) no one, some

6 Complete the short texts below with *some, any, no,* and their compounds.

   a On holidays _____ likes staying at home. Some people take trips, visit friends, or relatives. Other people prefer to go camping. Sometimes the parks are crowded, but people do not mind.

   b The young man heard a cry and turned around, but he could not see _____. At the same moment, a boy ran up to him and pointed towards the river.

   c **A:** Did you buy _____ overseas?

      B: Just a few souvenirs. I didn't buy _____ of value.

   d _____ was ready now, so we sat down. It was very peaceful in the cool grass – until we heard the noise of a hundred sheep coming down the hill towards us.

   e Driving along a highway one dark night, Steve had a flat tire. Suddenly _____ stopped. To his surprise, a well-dressed young lady got out and offered him her own spare tire.

   f Jason's parents took him to a big toy store on Saturday, but Jason found _____ wrong with _____ he saw. His parents showed him toy after toy, but he saw _____ he liked.

7 Answer these questions using *nobody, nothing, nowhere,* or *none.*

   a What can you do for me?

   _____

   b Where are you going?

   _____

   c Who did you meet?

   _____

   d How many bags are you carrying today?

   _____

8 Write full sentences that answer the questions in exercise 7. The first one is done for you.

   a *I can't do anything for you.*

   b _____

   c _____

   d _____

Reading

Areas of Physical and Economic Water Scarcity

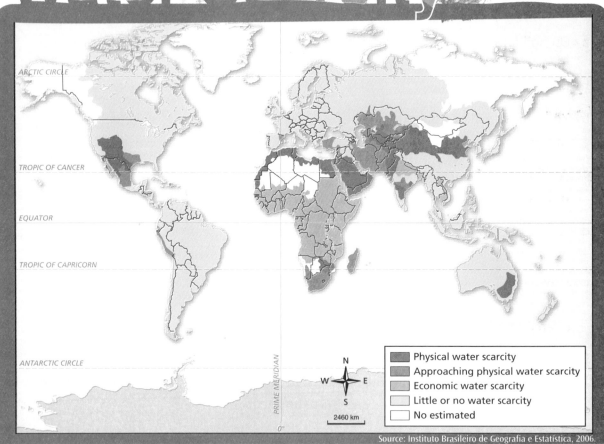

Legend:
- Physical water scarcity
- Approaching physical water scarcity
- Economic water scarcity
- Little or no water scarcity
- No estimated

2460 km

Source: Instituto Brasileiro de Geografia e Estatística, 2006.

- *Little or no water scarcity.* Abundant water resources relative to use, with less than 25% of water from rivers withdrawn for human purposes.

- *Physical water scarcity (water resources development is approaching or has exceeded sustainable limits).* More than 75% of the river flows are withdrawn for agriculture, industry, and domestic purposes (accounting for recycling of return flows). This definition – relating water availability to water demand – implies that dry areas are not necessarily water scarce.

- *Approaching physical water scarcity.* More than 60% of river flows are withdrawn. These basins will experience physical water scarcity in the near future.

- *Economic water scarcity (human, institutional, and financial capital limit access to water even though water in nature is available locally to meet human demands).* Water resources are abundant relative to water use, with less than 25% of water from rivers withdrawn for human purposes, but malnutrition exists.

Source: UN-water, 2007.
Extracted from <http://timeforchange.org/water-scarcity-and-global-warming>. Accessed on December 13, 2009.

basins: regiões banhadas por rios e seus afluentes

flows: escoamentos

has exceeded: excedeu

implies: significa, sugere

purposes: finalidades

scarcity: escassez

withdrawn: extraída, retirada

After Reading

1 Look at the map on page 124 and choose the right option.

  1.1 According to the text, water scarcity...

    a ( ) is increasing more in rich countries than in poor countries.

    b ( ) can be found in rich and poor countries.

    c ( ) will become a serious problem in the distant future.

  1.2 Which of the following water-related problems is mentioned in the text?

    a ( ) Malnutrition

    b ( ) Allergies

    c ( ) Intoxication

2 Study the words related to water on page 168. Then complete the sentences below.

  a I simply hate _____ coffee! I think I'll have some hot chocolate instead.

  b I prefer to buy _____ tablets because I don't like to swallow pills.

  c According to the club director, the _____ for the summer will be normal.

  d John got a new _____ watch on his birthday.

  e There are a lot of _____ areas in the state because of its dry weather.

  f Can you tell me where the _____ is? I'm very thirsty.

  g The village is famous for its spectacular _____ which attract lots of nature lovers.

Appendix 7
page 168

3 The map you can find on page 124 shows the effects of water scarcity all over the world. Match the countries and the types of water scarcity.

  a Physical water scarcity   ( ) Canada

  b Approaching physical water scarcity   ( ) The USA

  c Economic water scarcity   ( ) Brazil

  d Little or no water scarcity   ( ) Italy

  e Not estimated   ( ) China

     ( ) Argentina

Language in Action

1 Listen to part of an environmental engineer's speech about what people can do at home in order to save water. Write T (true) or F (false).

a (   ) Cooking, cleaning, washing, and drinking cause major water consumption.

b (   ) Consumption in the laundry involves water and detergents only.

c (   ) It is easy to save water if you install an efficient showerhead.

d (   ) A slowly leaking tap can waste more than 1,000 liters a month.

e (   ) There is no way to reuse grey water.

2 The chairman of the community center in your neighborhood is researching what people have been doing at home to reduce water consumption. Read the dialogue between the chairman and one of your neighbors.

A: What have you been doing to reduce water consumption?

B: We have been using some rainwater to wash the garage.

Now it's your turn!

Talk to a classmate. Use the Picture Dictionary 7 on page 162 to help you.

page 162

Writing

In small groups, make two lists: what you can do to reduce water consumption at home and at school. Use the vocabulary studied in this unit. Think of different actions as well.

PEDRO GENTILE

Consultando outras fontes

documentário: *A viagem da água* (Brasil; adaptação de Francisco César Filho para a edição do SMAS de Oeiras e Amadora; Escola Secundária Professor Ruy Luís Gomes, 2007). Disponível em <http://www.cienciamao.if.usp.br/tudo/exibir.php?midia=von&cod=_biologiaecologiaaviagemd>. Acessado em 3 de março de 2010.

livros: *Água – origem, uso e preservação* (Moderna, 2003; autor: Samuel Murgel Branco)

O atlas da água (Publifolha, 2006; autores: Robin Clarke e Jannet King)

música: "Planeta Água" (Guilherme Arantes). Letra e vídeo disponíveis em <http://letras.terra.com.br/guilherme-arantes/46315>. Acessado em 3 de março de 2010.

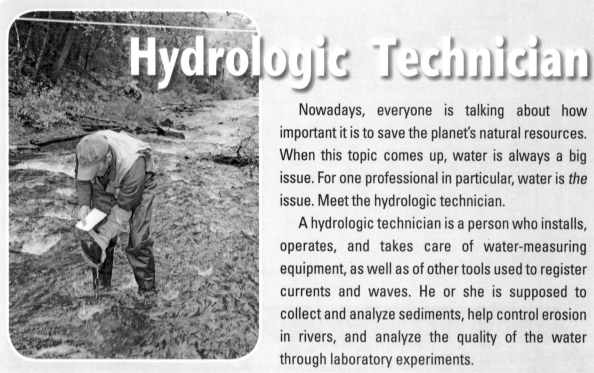

Hydrologic Technician

Nowadays, everyone is talking about how important it is to save the planet's natural resources. When this topic comes up, water is always a big issue. For one professional in particular, water is *the* issue. Meet the hydrologic technician.

A hydrologic technician is a person who installs, operates, and takes care of water-measuring equipment, as well as of other tools used to register currents and waves. He or she is supposed to collect and analyze sediments, help control erosion in rivers, and analyze the quality of the water through laboratory experiments.

A hydrologic technician is also in charge of organizing and participating in campaigns and projects that will help people make better use of water resources in their area.

These professionals may work for hydraulic and basic health care companies, or as environmental consultants.

In order to become a hydrologic technician, there is a thousand-hour course (approximately two years) you have to take.

Based on <http://www.usgs.gov/ohr/student/learn/jobs/job-hydro.html>;
<http://www.careerplanner.com/DOT-Job-Descriptions/HYDROLOGIST.cfm>;
<http://education-portal.com/search/quicksearch.html>;
<http://my.monster.com/job-profiles/Hydrologist.aspx?keyword=hydrology%20technician&re=1000>;
<http://www.wisegeek.com/what-is-hydrology.htm>.
Accessed on March 27, 2010.

comes up: surge
currents: correntes
issue: problema

water-measuring equipment: equipamento de medição de água
resources: recursos
waves: ondas

Para mais informações, acesse:

<http://catalogonct.mec.gov.br/et_infraestrutura/t_hidrologia.php>;

<http://www.centropaulasouza.sp.gov.br/Cursos/ETE/hidrologia.html>;

<http://www.iph.ufrgs.br/cth>;

<http://www.brasilprofissoes.com.br/verprof.php?codigo=218>.

1 Você gostaria de ser técnico em hidrologia? Por quê? / Por que não?

2 Study the photos below. Then match the instruments to their purpose in a hydrologic technician's routine.

pressure sensor

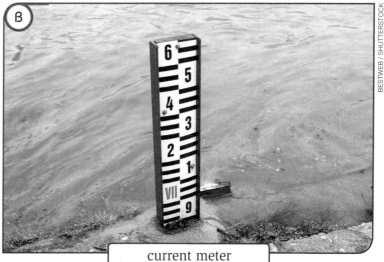

current meter

barometer

hygrometer

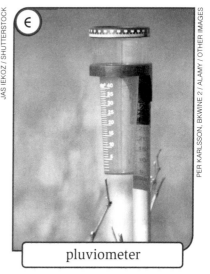

pluviometer

( ) instrument for measuring water velocity

( ) instrument for measuring the humidity of the air or of other gases

( ) instrument for measuring the pressure of gases or liquids

( ) instrument for measuring the atmospheric pressure

( ) instrument for measuring the amount of liquid precipitation

Additional Practice

For exercises 1 to 8, choose the best alternative.

1 A: Where's that delicious pasta you made for lunch? I'd like to have _____ for dinner.

B: There isn't _____ left.

a ( ) some; some
b ( ) any; something
c ( ) some; none
d ( ) some; any
e ( ) any; nothing

2 A: I'm kind of worried about Samantha. Do you know where she is?

B: Sorry, I have _____ idea.

a ( ) none
b ( ) some
c ( ) any
d ( ) anything
e ( ) no

3 A: I've heard a noise. I think _____ is at the door.

B: No, there isn't _____ there. It may have been the neighbor's cat again.

a ( ) anybody; somebody
b ( ) anyone; someone
c ( ) none; anybody
d ( ) somebody; anybody
e ( ) someone; somebody

4 A: What's the matter?

B: I can't find my wallet _____.

a ( ) somewhere
b ( ) anywhere
c ( ) someone
d ( ) none
e ( ) some

5 A: Did you know that 97% of all the world's water is salty or otherwise _____?

B: Yeah! And another 2% is frozen as ice caps and glaciers. That leaves only 1% for all of our needs!

a ( ) treated
b ( ) protected
c ( ) renewable
d ( ) unthinkable
e ( ) undrinkable

6 A: What else can we do to save water?

B: Well, have you heard about reusing _____?

a ( ) clean water
b ( ) grey water
c ( ) new water
d ( ) watery
e ( ) waterless

7 A: Man, don't you think you need a new car?

B: Absolutely, but I can't _____ a new car at the moment. I'm still paying for university.

a ( ) concern
b ( ) afford
c ( ) ensure
d ( ) income
e ( ) discharge

8 A: What's going on? I've never seen so many students together.

B: It's an assembly. The director has called all of them to _____ they are going to come up with the proper decision.

a ( ) push
b ( ) help
c ( ) ensure

d ( ) discharge

e ( ) improve

9 Choose the alternative that best completes the lyrics "These Days", by REM.

I had a hat I put it down and it sunk, reached down,

Yanked it up, slapped it on my head

All the people gather

Fly to carry each his _____

Extracted from <http://www.lyricsera.com/239779-lyric-Rem-These+Days.html>.
Accessed on February 26, 2010.

a ( ) ensure

b ( ) improve

c ( ) afford

d ( ) income

e ( ) burden

10 Choose the alternative that best completes the lyrics "Somebody to Love", by Queen.

[...]

Every day I try and I try and I try

But _____ wants to put me down

They say I'm going crazy

They say I got a lot of water in my brain

Got no common sense

I got _____ left to believe

Yeah yeah yeah yeah

[...]

Extracted from <http://www.lyrics007.com/Queen%20Lyrics/
Somebody%20To%20Love%20Lyrics.html>.
Accessed on February 26, 2010.

a ( ) nobody, anybody

b ( ) everybody, anybody

c ( ) anybody, anybody

d ( ) everybody, nobody

e ( ) everybody, somebody

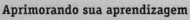

Refletindo sobre sua aprendizagem

Ao final desta unidade, você já é capaz de:

- Localizar os oceanos no mapa-múndi. ☐
- Produzir adjetivos a partir do acréscimo do prefixo *un-*, traduzir esses adjetivos e usá-los em diferentes contextos. ☐
- Distinguir problemas e soluções relacionados ao meio ambiente. ☐
- Reconhecer e empregar corretamente *some*, *any*, *no* e seus compostos em diferentes situações comunicativas. ☐
- Fazer leitura e depreender informações de mapas. ☐
- Interpretar e utilizar expressões formadas com a palavra *water*. ☐
- Associar informações entre texto oral e texto escrito. ☐
- Usar a linguagem oral para colocar-se como agente transformador diante do problema da falta de água. ☐
- Produzir listas referentes às atitudes que podem ser tomadas para reduzir o consumo de água. ☐

Aprimorando sua aprendizagem

- Peça ajuda ao professor ou aos colegas para que esclareçam suas dúvidas.
- Refaça os exercícios.
- Visite a biblioteca da sua escola ou uma biblioteca pública e consulte livros de gramática e/ou faça leituras de seu interesse.
- Assista a filmes em inglês.

PEDRO GENTILE

Reprodução proibida. Art. 184 do Código Penal e Lei 9.610 de 19 de fevereiro de 1998.

PRE-READING

Look at the title. What is the main idea of the text?

File   Edit   View   Favorites   Tools   Help

Address   http://www.survivalinternational.org/tribes/brazilian#main   Go   Links »

The Brazilian Indians

Five hundred years of exposure to disease, violence, and dispossession wiped out the vast majority of this indigenous population. Today, there are around 650,000 Indians in Brazil in over 200 tribes, who live scattered across the country.

Among them they speak a huge number of languages; 110 of the tribal languages of Brazil have fewer than 400 speakers. [...]

How do they live?

Brazil's tribal peoples live in a wide range of environments – tropical forests, grasslands, scrub forests, and semi-deserts – and have a wide range of ways of life.

Their experience of contact with European invaders and their descendants also varies widely: some, such as the Guarani in the south, have been in contact with white people for 500 years; others encountered them far more recently; and some tribes are effectively uncontacted – the majority of the world's uncontacted tribes, probably more than 50, live in Brazil.

Most tribes live by a mixture of hunting, gathering, and growing plants for food, medicine, and to make everyday objects. Probably only the uncontacted Awá and Maku are completely nomadic, living entirely by hunting and gathering in the Amazon.

What problems do they face?

In the 500 years since Europeans arrived in Brazil, the tribal peoples there have experienced genocide on a huge scale, and the loss of much of their land.

Today, their land is still taken over for ranches or industrial projects, or invaded by miners and settlers – and they are still being killed, whether by diseases encountered when their lands are invaded, by starvation as they are driven from their hunting grounds, or by the hitmen who are employed by ranchers and 'landowners' to keep Indians away.

There remains an endemic racism towards Indians in Brazil that makes all this possible – in law they are still considered minors. The most important thing for tribal peoples in Brazil is control over their lands – Brazil is one of only two South American countries that does not recognize tribal land ownership.

If Brazil's tribes were recognized as the owners of their land, it would give them some real protection against the individuals and businesses that take over their land, destroying their livelihood and often destroying them.

Start

Extracted from <http://www.survivalinternational.org/tribes/brazilian#main>. Accessed on December 14, 2009.

dispossession: desapropriação
encountered: encontraram
gathering: coleta, colheita
grounds: áreas
growing: plantação

hitmen: matadores de aluguel, pistoleiros
livelihood: sustento
nomadic: nômades
ranches: fazendas

scattered: dispersos
settlers: colonos
starvation: fome
uncontacted: isoladas
wide range: gama, grande variedade

After Reading

1 Write T (true) or F (false). Correct the false statements.

a ( ) Brazilian Indians have been exposed to many diseases and much violence in the last 500 years.

_____

b ( ) All 200 Brazilian Indian tribes live together in a special protected area.

_____

c ( ) Among them, all Indians speak the same language.

_____

d ( ) Most of the world's uncontacted tribes are in Brazil.

_____

2 Answer the questions.

a What are some of the main problems Indians in Brazil have had since Europeans invaded their lands?

_____

b Where do Brazil's tribes live?

_____

c Which Amazonian tribes live exclusively by hunting and gathering?

_____

3 Leia o extrato de texto abaixo e discuta-o com seus colegas.

> [...] No que diz respeito à identidade étnica, as mudanças ocorridas em várias sociedades indígenas, como o fato de falarem português, vestirem roupas iguais às dos outros membros da sociedade nacional com que estão em contato, utilizarem modernas tecnologias (como câmeras de vídeo, máquinas fotográficas e aparelhos de fax), não fazem com que percam sua identidade étnica e deixem de ser indígenas [...]

Extraído de <http://www.funai.gov.br>.
Acessado em 23 de fevereiro de 2010.

a Em sua opinião, é necessário reconhecer e valorizar a identidade étnica específica de cada uma das sociedades indígenas, compreendendo suas línguas e suas formas tradicionais de organização social, de ocupação da terra e de uso dos recursos naturais?

b Baseado nas informações contidas no texto, você concorda com a afirmação de que as sociedades indígenas não estão perdendo sua identidade étnica?

Vocabulary in Use

Phrasal verbs are usually two-word phrases consisting of *verb + preposition* or *verb + adverb*. Their meaning is different from the verb itself.

1 Match the phrasal verbs in bold with the best definition.

a All kinds of violence **wiped out** the vast majority of this indigenous population.

b "Most tribes **live by** a mixture of hunting, gathering, and growing plants for food, …"

c Hitmen are hired by ranchers and 'landowners' to **keep** Indians **away**.

d It would give them real protection against the ones that **take over** their lands.

e Don't **give up** on me.

f The teacher is going to **hand out** the exams.

g Amanda's father is going to be mad when he **finds out** she got a tattoo.

( ) assume control of something
( ) to maintain at a distance
( ) kill all of a population, destroy
( ) follow a particular belief
( ) stop trying to do something
( ) discover
( ) distribute

Appendix 8

page 168

2 Complete the sentences below with the correct phrasal verbs from exercise 1. Make all the necessary changes.

a Can you _____ what time the play starts?

b We should _____ the party fliers in the evening.

c _____ the kids _____ from the oven.

d Who is going to _____ the family business when Carlos's grandmother retires?

e Jacob _____ his swimming classes last week. He's going to attend karate classes instead.

f The wave _____ the fishing village.

g Being vegetarian is a way of life I could _____.

3 Now choose three phrasal verbs from exercise 2 and write your own sentences.

a _____

b _____

c _____

Grammar in Use

RELATIVE PRONOUNS

Os **relative pronouns** unem uma oração ao seu antecedente, um substantivo. Eles introduzem as orações que indicam a qual pessoa, objeto, animal ou ideia o locutor se refere.

Who refere-se a pessoas.	The Indians **who** live in Brazil speak a huge number of languages.
Whom refere-se a pessoas. É utilizado quando o pronome relativo for objeto do verbo. Após preposições.	A native Indian leader **whom** I look up to is Raoni. Raoni was the Caiapó tribe chief with **whom** the famous singer Sting worked on behalf of Xingu National Park.
Which refere-se a animais, objetos e ideias.	The Indian tribes **which** are effectively uncontacted live by hunting and gathering in the Amazon.
Whose indica relação de posse. É seguido por um substantivo e nunca pode ser omitido.	The Indian tribes **whose** values were learned from their ancestors believe we should preserve the Earth.
That refere-se a pessoas, objetos e/ou animais. É utilizado após superlativos e palavras como **some**, **any**, **no**, **everything**, **much**, **little**, **only** e **all**. Não é usado entre vírgulas.	The rainforest **that** we consider the biggest reserve in the world is Xingu National Park.
Where é usado como pronome relativo para se referir a lugares.	The environments **where** Brazil's tribal peoples live are tropical forests, grasslands, scrub forests, and semi-deserts.
When refere-se a dia, mês, etc.	My mom still remembers **when** I started to walk.
What refere-se a objetos, assuntos – algo determinado.	My brother didn't talk about **what** had happened yesterday.

1 Circle the relative pronouns in the cartoons below.

The guy who collected vinyl

"Hey, I think that animal that chewed us up
might have been some kind of bear!"

"This is the planet where nachos rule."

2 Match the columns to form sentences.

a Our planet is endangered by people…

b The chief,…

c Activists…

d Indians want their own lands…

e There are a few Indians…

( ) who is the ruler of the tribe, governs based on his ancestors' guidance.

( ) where they can live in peace with nature.

( ) who support the idea that they should adapt to other cultures.

( ) who don't have any respect towards nature.

( ) whose cause is the environment are interested in Raoni's fight.

3 Choose the best relative pronouns to complete the sentences. More than one answer might be correct.

3.1 Are we the kind of parents _____ they're talking about?

a ( ) who   b ( ) that   c ( ) which   d ( ) Ø

3.2 That is the school _____ my son will study.

a ( ) who   b ( ) where   c ( ) whose   d ( ) Ø

3.3 The pet _____ the children love is the dog.

a ( ) who   b ( ) which   c ( ) what   d ( ) Ø

3.4 The wife _____ husband is in jail is waiting for me outside.

a ( ) whose   b ( ) where   c ( ) who   d ( ) Ø

3.5 There are artists about _____ we've never written.

a ( ) who   b ( ) that   c ( ) whom   d ( ) Ø

3.6 I love the movie *I Know _____ You Did Last Summer*.

a ( ) *Which*   b ( ) *What*   c ( ) *Whose*   d ( ) Ø

3.7 The singer answered all the interviewer's questions, _____ came as a great surprise.

a ( ) what   b ( ) which   c ( ) who   d ( ) Ø

3.8 White, _____ has become popular again this summer, is mandatory in bikinis and beach shorts.

a ( ) that   b ( ) which   c ( ) whom   d ( ) Ø

4 Join the sentences using relative pronouns.

a Bernard is my student. He loves reading.

_____

b He wrote me a letter. It was a love poem.

_____

c The musician played wonderfully. She performed all night.

_____

d I met an old man. His son was a doctor at the university hospital.

_____

e The night club was crowded. They celebrated their anniversary there.

_____

f The girl is lovely. We've been looking at her for hours.

_____

5 Read the review of *The Silence of the Lambs* written by a student. Complete the review with relative pronouns.

[…] The Silence of the Lambs' bases on a novel by Thomas Harris and has become one of the most famous films of all time. The main person is Clarice Starling (Jodie Foster), a young detective _____ job it is to solve the mystery. To do this, she has to interrogate a notorious killer, Hannibal the Cannibal, _____ plays by Anthony Hopkins. The plot is absolutely good – on the one side it is a suspense thriller and on the other an intelligent analysis of the criminal mind. Furthermore, it not only focuses on the chase for the killer himself, but also on the psychological battle _____ takes place between Foster and Hopkins. Besides there is a lot of violence, it is never gratuitous. […]

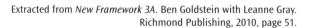

Extracted from *New Framework 3A*. Ben Goldstein with Leanne Gray. Richmond Publishing, 2010, page 51.

6 Read the plot summaries of the films below. Identify the relative pronouns and underline the words they refer to.

Slumdog Millionaire is the story of Jamal Malik (Patel), an 18 year-old orphan from the slums of Mumbai, who is about to experience the biggest day of his life. With the whole nation watching, he is just one question away from winning a staggering 20 million rupees on India's *Who Wants To Be a Millionaire?* But when the show breaks for the night, police arrest him on suspicion of cheating; how could a street kid know so much? Desperate to prove his innocence, Jamal tells the story of his life in the slum where he and his brother grew up, of their adventures together on the road, of vicious encounters with local gangs, and of Latika (Pinto), the girl he loved and lost. Each chapter of his story reveals the key to the answer to one of the game show's questions. [...]

Extracted from <http://www.imdb.com/title/tt1010048/synopsis>.
Accessed on February 24, 2010.

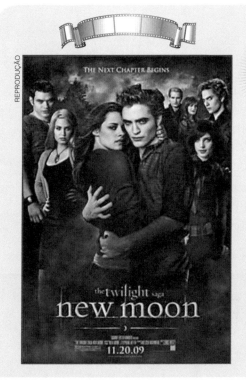

After Bella recovers from the vampire attack that almost claimed her life, she looks to celebrate her birthday with Edward and his family. However, a minor accident during the festivities results in Bella's blood being shed, a sight that proves too intense for the Cullens, who decide to leave the town of Forks, Washington, for Bella and Edward's sake. Initially heartbroken, Bella finds a form of comfort in reckless living, as well as an even-closer friendship with Jacob Black. Danger in different forms awaits.

Extracted from <http://www.imdb.com/title/tt1259571/plotsummary>.
Accessed on February 24, 2010.

Reading

THE APURINA PEOPLE

Who Are the Apurina?

The Apurina people live along the river Purus and its tributaries in the Brazilian Amazon. They belong to the linguistic group Aruak and call themselves in their own language "Popingaré" or "Kangitê". Currently they are spread over 23 indigenous territories in the Brazilian state of Amazonas with a population of 2416 (Funai 1987). One of these communities is known as "Apurina of the 45". They are located at the 45 km point on the BR-317 highway between Boca do Acre in the state of Amazonas and Rio Branco in the state of Acre.

Rural Exodus

Depending on market economy, some of the Apurina migrate to the suburbs of Boca do Acre and Rio Branco in search of new opportunities, leaving behind their indigenous identity. This rural exodus threatens legal maintenance and environmental protection of their demarcated indigenous lands. [...]

Extracted from <http://www.amazonlink.org/apurina/engl/index.htm>.
Accessed on December 21, 2009.

THE KUIKURO

WHAT THE REGION IS LIKE TODAY

The Kuikuro people were active participants in the author's fieldwork and co-authors on the resulting journal articles. Theirs is one of the few Amazonian societies to maintain the full breadth of its culture – language, rituals, art – despite centuries of depopulation, and they continue to practice intensive agriculture (mostly of manioc), fish farming, orchard production, and forest management.

Extracted from *Scientific American*, October 2009, p. 67.

currently: no presente
demarcated: demarcada
in search of: em busca de
indigenious: nativos

maintenance: permanência
threatens: ameaça
tributaries: afluentes

After Reading

1 Choose the best alternative according to the text **The Apurina People**.

    1.1 Where do the Apurina People live?

        a ( ) They live far from the river Purus and its tributaries in the Brazilian Amazon.

        b ( ) They live along the river Purus and its tributaries in the Brazilian Amazon.

        c ( ) They all live between Boca do Acre in the state of Amazonas and Rio Branco in the state of Acre.

    1.2 Where can they be found nowadays?

        a ( ) They are spread over 23 indigenous territories in Amazonas.

        b ( ) They are spread over territories in Acre.

        c ( ) They are spread over 23 indigenous territories between Boca do Acre in the state of Amazonas and Rio Branco in the state of Acre.

    1.3 Why do some of them migrate?

        a ( ) They migrate to the suburbs of Boca do Acre and Rio Branco in search of studies.

        b ( ) They migrate to the suburbs of Boca do Acre and Rio Branco in search of homes.

        c ( ) They migrate to the suburbs of Boca do Acre and Rio Branco in search of new opportunities.

    1.4 What kind of problems can be caused by this rural exodus?

        a ( ) The rural exodus improves legal maintenance and environmental protection of their demarcated indigenous lands.

        b ( ) The rural exodus threatens legal maintenance and environmental protection of their demarcated indigenous lands.

        c ( ) The rural exodus maintains legal maintenance and environmental protection of their demarcated indigenous lands.

2 Read the text **The Kuikuro** once again and find the corresponding words in English.

    a trabalho de campo (line 2)   _____

    b amplitude (line 4)   _____

    c despovoamento (line 5)   _____

    d mandioca (line 6)   _____

    e cultivo de peixe (lines 6/7)   _____

    f pomar (line 7)   _____

Language in Action

1 Marcelo's family is from the Northeast of Brazil. They have been living in Colorado, U.S., for six months. It's dinner time. They're listening to an interview on a local radio station about the isolated indigenous peoples of Brazil. Listen to the interview and complete the information below.

a There are _____ groups of isolated Indians in Brazil today.

b They live in the states of Acre, Amazonas, _____, Mato Gosso, Pará,

_____,

and Roraima.

c The isolated indigenous groups hunt, _____, and collect fruits and _____.

d They live a semi-nomadic existence and avoid _____ with other indigenous groups as well as with non-Indians.

e It is not known what _____ they speak.

2 Talk to a classmate about the text on page 132. Ask questions using the cues given.

> How many / tribes / in Brazil / today
> What languages / Indians / speak
> How / they / live
> What / they / usually do
> Why / their land / taken over

Writing

page 163

The Yanomamis are one of the most numerous and best-known tribes in South America. Write a paragraph about them. Use the photo and the information given to help you.

_____

_____

_____

_____

_____

_____

_____

_____

◆ One of the largest relatively isolated tribes in South America.

◆ In the rainforests and mountains of northern Brazil and southern Venezuela.

◆ Population: around 32,000.

◆ Area: the largest forested indigenous territory in the world.

◆ Threats: cattle ranchers invading and deforesting the eastern border of their land; gold-miners working illegally on their land.

◆ Way of life: live in large, circular, communal houses called _yanos_ or _shabonos_.

◆ Belief: equality among people.

◆ Organization: decisions by consensus during long debates.

◆ Tasks: divided between the sexes.

PHOTO: ROSA GAUDITANO / STUDIO R; ILLUSTRATIONS: MILTON RODRIGUES ALVES; ART: PEDRO GENTILE

Consultando outras fontes

documentário: _Os Kuikuro se apresentam. Projeto vídeo nas aldeias._ Kuhi Ikugü. Disponível em: <http://www.videonasaldeias.org.br/2009>. Acessado em 3 de março de 2010.

livros: _Lendas e mitos dos índios brasileiros_ (FTD, 1998; autor: Waldemar de Andrade e Silva)

Xingu – Os índios seus mitos (Zahar, 1990; autor: Orlando Villas Boas e Cláudio Villas Boas)

Community Technician

The career of a community technician is, above all, about communicating with others.

Community technicians are the ones who take part in different kinds of activities which help a community to interact better. These individuals help foster a democratic attitude that prioritizes the actions a community wants to take. A community technician works under the careful supervision of a professional in the social area. Together, they help develop a strong community leadership. He or she also participates in educational campaigns and works towards improving people's lifestyle and preserving their culture.

A community technician may work in private or public institutions, such as community associations or syndicates. He or she can also work with multidisciplinary teams in order to make projects that aim for sustainable development.

If you are willing to be a community technician, you will have to take an 800-hour course.

Based on <http://www.digiops.org.nz/projects/currentprojects/communitytechnicians>;
<http://online.onetcenter.org/link/summary/11-9151.00>;
<http://www.careerplanner.com/Job-Descriptions/Forest-and-Conservation-Technicians.cfm>;
<http://www.job-search-engine.com/keyword/community-technician>;
<http://www.universities.com/edu/Western_Iowa_Tech_Community_College.html>.
Accessed on February 6, 2010.

Para mais informações, acesse:

<http://catalogonct.mec.gov.br/et_apoio_educacional/t_orientacao_comunitaria.php>;

<http://www.litoral.ufpr.br/htms/em_toc/toc.htm>;

<http://www.diaadia.pr.gov.br/cge/arquivos/File/PPP_ufpr.pdf>.

1 Você gostaria de ser técnico em orientação comunitária? Por quê? / Por que não?

2 Match the words to the definitions. Then associate the words with the pictures below.

a computer lab	( ) a place where people keep books
b library	( ) a multifunctional machine that can be taken anywhere
c calculator	( ) a device used for conversations
d desktop computer	( ) a place where there are a lot of computers you can use temporarily
e notebook	( ) a machine composed of four pieces: a monitor, a keyboard, a mouse, and a CPU
f telephone	( ) a device that makes Math a whole lot easier

300DPI / SHUTTERSTOCK

STOCK CONNECTION DISTRIBUTION / ALAMY / OTHER IMAGES

RAFA IRUSTA / SHUTTERSTOCK

ARTUR SYNENKO / SHUTTERSTOCK

STILLFX / SHUTTERSTOCK

MARWOOD JENKINS / ALAMY / OTHER IMAGES

Additional Practice

For exercises 1 to 7, choose the best alternative.

1 Ted came here yesterday. He came with a friend _____ studies with him at the new school.

- **a** ( ) which
- **b** ( ) who
- **c** ( ) whose
- **d** ( ) whom
- **e** ( ) what

2 **Ryan:** I don't know what's going on. I can't make this camera work!

Zack: To take a picture you must press the shutter button, _____ is on the top of the camera.

- **a** ( ) who
- **b** ( ) whose
- **c** ( ) when
- **d** ( ) which
- **e** ( ) whom

3 **Emma:** That is the bank _____ was robbed.

Mia: How do you know that?

Emma: Paul, _____ sister is in my class, was there. He said the thief _____ robbed the bank was carrying two guns and was wearing a mask _____ made him look like Frankenstein!

- **a** ( ) who; whom, that, when
- **b** ( ) when; where, who, whose
- **c** ( ) that; whom, which, whose
- **d** ( ) that; whose, who, which
- **e** ( ) whose; which, who, whom

4 "Paul Goossens faced many dangerous men _____ came to ask him for special or unusual guns, but there was something particularly cold and frightening about the visitor from England [...]"

Extracted from *The Day of the Jackal*, by Frederick Forsyth, Pearson Education Limited, 1999. p. 13.

- **a** ( ) where
- **b** ( ) whom
- **c** ( ) which
- **d** ( ) who
- **e** ( ) whose

5 The theory about the extinction of the dinosaurs is that a meteor crashing into our planet _____ them _____.

- **a** ( ) wiped, out
- **b** ( ) took, over
- **c** ( ) kept, away
- **d** ( ) gave, up
- **e** ( ) lived, by

6 Not everybody actually _____ his or her religious convictions.

- **a** ( ) hands out
- **b** ( ) finds out
- **c** ( ) keeps away
- **d** ( ) wipes out
- **e** ( ) lives by

7 This Physics homework is difficult, but I won't _____ doing it.

- **a** ( ) take over
- **b** ( ) give up
- **c** ( ) hand out
- **d** ( ) wipe out
- **e** ( ) find out

From exercises 8 to 10, choose the alternative that best completes each extract of the lyrics below.

8 "Day Tripper" by The Beatles:

[...]

She was a day tripper, one way ticket, yeah!
It took me so long to _____, and I

_____.

[...]

a ( ) found out, find out
b ( ) find out, finds out
c ( ) find out, found out
d ( ) finds out, finds out
e ( ) found out, found out

Extracted from <http://www.sing365.com/music/lyric.nsf/
day-tripper-lyrics-the-beatles/8c0a1e1fa6d226f548256bc2001d2794>.
Accessed on February 28, 2010.

9 "Speed of Sound" by Coldplay:

[...]

The sign _____ I couldn't read,
Or a light _____ I couldn't see,
Some things you have to believe,
But others are puzzles, puzzling me.

[...]

a ( ) who, who
b ( ) whom, that
c ( ) whose, whose
d ( ) when, when
e ( ) that, that

Extracted from <http://www.azlyrics.com/lyrics/coldplay/
speedofsound.html>.
Accessed on February 28, 2010.

10 "The Man Who Can't Be Moved" by The Script:

Going back to the corner _____ I first saw you,
Gonna camp in my sleeping bag, I'm not gonna move.
Got some words on cardboard, got your picture in my hand
Saying, "If you see this girl, can you tell her where I am?"

Extracted from <http://www.elyrics.net/read/s/script-lyrics/
the-man-who-can_t-be-moved-lyrics.html>.
Accessed on February 28, 2010.

a ( ) which
b ( ) what
c ( ) where
d ( ) who
e ( ) whose

✓

Refletindo sobre sua aprendizagem

Ao final desta unidade, você já é capaz de:

- Refletir e colocar-se criticamente em relação às recentes mudanças sociais e culturais indígenas. ▢
- Reconhecer a formação de *phrasal verbs*, o significado de alguns deles e seu uso em diferentes contextos. ▢
- Reconhecer a função dos pronomes relativos como elementos coesivos em diferentes textos. ▢
- Identificar os elementos aos quais se relacionam os pronomes relativos. ▢
- Localizar palavras específicas no texto a partir de seu significado em português. ▢
- Depreender informações, fazer inferências e estabelecer semelhanças e diferenças por meio da leitura de imagens. ▢
- Elaborar perguntas e respostas com base em um texto. ▢
- Expandir seu conhecimento sobre uma tribo indígena brasileira e produzir um texto organizado a partir de informações escritas e visuais. ▢

Aprimorando sua aprendizagem

- Peça ajuda ao professor ou aos colegas para que esclareçam suas dúvidas.
- Refaça os exercícios.
- Visite a biblioteca da sua escola ou uma biblioteca pública e consulte livros de gramática e/ou faça leituras de seu interesse.
- Assista a filmes em inglês.

1 Look at the pictures below. Write the names of the food.

2 Complete the table with the words in exercise 1.

Countable Nouns		Uncountable Nouns
Singular	Plural	Singular only
carrot	carrots	cereal

3 Complete the sentences about the food in exercise 1.

a There's some _____, _____, _____, and _____.

b There are some _____, _____, _____, _____, and _____.

c There is one _____.

d There _____ broccoli.

e There _____ olives.

4 Newton and his friend Bruno are getting ready to go camping. Use *some*, *any*, *no*, and *none* in the blanks provided to complete their dialogue.

Newton: Well, we'll need _____ maps, a compass, and _____ food.

Don't worry about it. I'm making a list. We'll take _____ bread and

_____ ham as well. We won't take _____ fruit.

Bruno: How about _____ juice?

Newton: We could buy four cartons of apple juice.

Bruno: But cartons are too heavy to carry around. I have _____ energy to carry a

lot of weight and walk long distances at the same time.

Newton: It's true, but we'll have to take _____ water with us.

Bruno: Shall we take some cash, too?

Newton: There won't be _____ stores nearby, but we'll need _____

money in case something goes wrong. If you have _____ medical

restrictions, we'd better know what they are.

Bruno: I have _____. Don't worry about me.

5 Underline the correct word.

5.1 Can I have **something** / **anything** to eat? I'm starving.

5.2 Would you like **some** / **no** more chocolate?

5.3 Please don't put **any** / **some** sugar in my coffee.

5.4 Peter rarely does **nothing** / **anything** on weekends.

5.5 Gisele is so wealthy she can go **anywhere** / **somewhere** she wants in her free time.

5.6 There is **some / no** use crying over spilled milk, is there?

5.7 What about asking **anyone / someone** for directions?

5.8 It's too late. **Nothing / Something** can be done about it at this moment.

6 Read parts of some lyrics. Complete them with the words in the box.

any (x2)   everybody   everyday   nobody   no one   somewhere

"Somebody to Love", Queen

[...]

_____ I try and I try and I try

But _____ wants to put me down

They say I'm going crazy

They say I got a lot of water in my brain

Ah, got no common sense

I got _____ left to believe in

Yeah yeah yeah yeah

[...]

"Any Other Day Lyrics", Hilary Duff

[...]

On a day like _____ other day

Sky's so blue it could take your, take your breathe away

'Cause I remember where I was when I heard the news

I remember where I was when I heard the news

I remember where I was

Sky's so blue like _____ other day

"Anywhere", Evanescence

[...]

I have dreamt of a place for you and I

_____ knows who we are there

All I want is to give my life only to you

I've dreamt so long I cannot dream anymore

Let's run away, I'll take you there

[...]

"Somewhere", Barbra Streisand

[...]

There's a place for us

A time and a place for us

Hold my hand and we're half way there

hold my hand and I'll take you there

Somehow,

someday, _____

[...]

7 Complete each of the following sentences with a phrasal verb that corresponds to the definition in parentheses.

a When Sarah arrived at the opening plenary, the speaker's assistant had already _____ (distributed) the notes.

b The headline of the newspaper revealed that whole villages had been _____ (destroyed) by the floods and the earthquake.

c People are wondering who's going to _____ (assume control) when the old dictator dies and the nation is free again.

d Sarah said that her family had always tried to _____ (follow a particular belief) their faith and their religion.

e Dad was furious when he _____ (discovered) where I was living.

f John _____ (stopped doing something) his job and started writing poetry.

g If I were you, I'd _____ (remain at a distance) from that area at night.

8 Join the sentences using relative pronouns.

a Susan's the girl. She works in the library.

_____

b Here's the alarm clock. I bought it yesterday.

_____

c I've spoken to John. His house was robbed last Monday.

_____

d There is the hospital. I was born there.

_____

e 1945 was the year. The Second World War ended then.

_____

f That is the man. I spoke to him after the class.

_____

Reading Labels
Cross-Curricular Connections: Chemistry, Arts

In small groups:

- Create a product to be exported.

- Think of as many details as possible, such as: What kind of product is it? Is it for children, teens, or adults? How many flavors is the product going to come in? Which ones? Where is it going to be sold? What is the brand name?

- Make a draft of the product on a separate sheet of paper.

- Make sentences based on the ones on the fruit juice packaging.

- Hand in the draft to your teacher for correction.

A Different Way of Volunteering

Cross-Curricular Connection: Sociology

Read the text and do the activity below.

Sews for the homeless. Mends more than clothes.

Shifra Mincer

VOLUNTEERING

Pass It On:

VALUES.COM THE FOUNDATION FOR A BETTER LIFE

Shifra Mincer, age 16, of New York, NY, is known as the Sewing Lady at a New York City soup kitchen, where for six years she has spent several hours each Monday night mending clothes for people who eat there. As a fifth-grader volunteering at the soup kitchen, Shifra realized she could use her sewing talent and passion to patch coats, repair tote bags, and sew on buttons for people who had no one else to help them with these tasks. Soup kitchen clients quickly came to know and love Shifra not just for her sewing but for her conversation, her humor, and her interest in their lives. "I became addicted to helping people," explains Shifra, and so she recently expanded her efforts to create a co-ed sewing club at her school. The club meets weekly to learn to sew and to work on projects (such as small heart-shaped pillows) for children and the elderly in New York City's shelters. "I will never be able to sew every homeless person's coat or mittens," says Shifra, "But the little part I do makes all the difference to that one person." Shifra was a 2003 winner of the Gloria Barron Prize.

Extracted from <http://www.montana.edu/hhunts/feelgood/young_people_step_up_to_keep_ame.htm>.
Accessed on February 19, 2010.

In small groups:

- Think of some ways you can help your neighborhood to protect the environment. Take personal talents into consideration.
- If you need some examples and have access to computers, check the Gloria Barron Prize site: <http://www.barronprize.org/index.html>.
- Prepare a poster explaining what you are going to do to help. Use photos or drawings to illustrate the poster.
- Present your ideas to your classmates. Invite them to take part in your project.

Brazilian Cartoonists

Cross-Curricular Connection: Arts

Read about two famous Brazilian cartoonists and do the activity below.

Ziraldo Alves Pinto started his career in the '50s. He is a graphic artist, a journalist, a playwright, a cartoonist, a caricaturist, and a writer.

In the '60s he launched the first Brazilian comic book made by a single author: *A turma do Pererê*. During the Military Years (1964-1984) he founded *O Pasquim*, a newspaper that generated a school of followers. His comics for adults, notably *Supermãe* and *Mineirinho: o Comequieto*, also have legions of fans.

Miguel Paiva began writing for publication at the age of sixteen. He is a cartoonist, an art director, a writer, a playwright, an illustrator, an advertising director, and a journalist in Brazil.

He has worked for *O Pasquim*. He has published many books in Brazil and abroad, such as *As memórias de Casanova*.

Miguel is also the author of the characters *Chiquinha*, published in *O Globo*, and *Bebel, the Top Top Model*, published in *Contigo!*.

In small groups:

- Do some research about one of the cartoonists above.
- Choose some comic strips he has produced and make copies.
- Display the comic strips on a piece of cardboard.
- Compare them to the ones produced by Mauricio de Sousa. How are they different? How are they similar?
- Show your poster to your classmates.
- Make an oral presentation of the conclusions you have come to.

Awesome Savings

Cross-Curricular Connections: Sociology, Science

Read the following tips for saving water and then do the activity below.

⊘ Never put water down the drain when there may be another use for it – such as watering a plant or garden, or cleaning.
[…]

⊘ Store drinking water in the refrigerator rather than letting the tap run every time you want a cool glass of water.
[…]

⊘ Do not use running water to thaw meat or other frozen foods. Defrost food overnight in the refrigerator or by using the defrost setting on your microwave.
[…]

⊘ Consider installing an instant water heater on your kitchen sink so you don't have to let the water run while it heats up. This will reduce heating costs for your household.
[…]

Extracted from <http://www.americanwater.com/49ways.htm>.
Accessed on February 24, 2010.

In small groups:

◯ Create an informative leaflet about the most useful tips on saving water for you, your friends, and your neighbors.

◯ Use photos and/or drawings to illustrate it.

◯ Take action: distribute your leaflet to your classmates and members of your community.

1

A New Food Pyramid Style

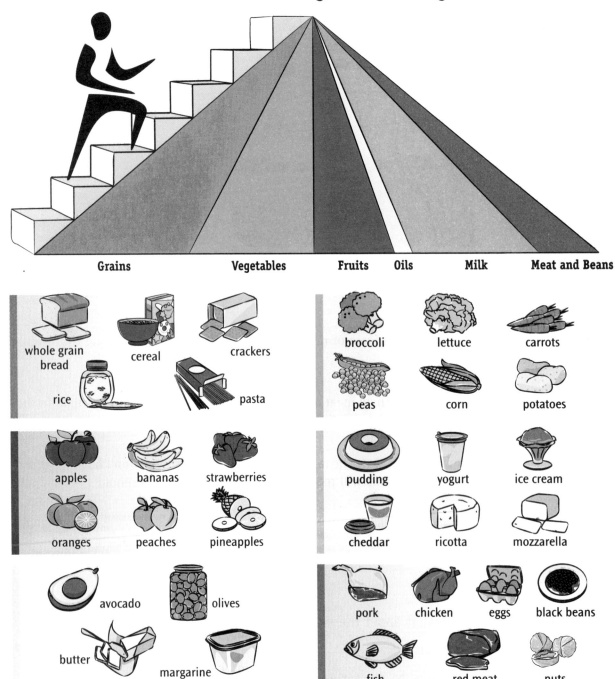

Grains   Vegetables   Fruits   Oils   Milk   Meat and Beans

whole grain bread
cereal
crackers
rice
pasta

broccoli
lettuce
carrots
peas
corn
potatoes

apples
bananas
strawberries
oranges
peaches
pineapples

pudding
yogurt
ice cream
cheddar
ricotta
mozzarella

avocado
olives
butter
margarine

pork
chicken
eggs
black beans
fish
red meat
nuts

Based on <http://www.mypyramid.gov/pyramid/index.html>.
Accessed on January 29, 2010.

The Amazon Is Great!

ILLUSTRATIONS: MILTON RODRIGUES ALVES

AMAZON
EXPLORING

Take a helicopter flight.

Take part in a jungle cruise.

Swim with the pink dolphins.

Go on a tour boat.

Enjoy local Indian traditions.

3
Making a Difference

Cleaning a park.

Helping the elderly in nursing homes.

Reading stories to children.

Recycling.

Collecting items for charity such as clothes, food, or furniture.

Participation in school activities that benefit the wider community.

4
Millennium Development Goals

End poverty and hunger

Universal education

Gender equality

Child health

Maternal health

Combat HIV/AIDS

Environmental sustainability

Global partnership

UNITED NATIONS 2010

5
Household Chores

Make the bed.

Take out the trash.

Dust the furniture.

Set the table.

Vacuum the floor.

Wash the clothes.

6
Comic Strip Sound Effects

7

Saving Water Attitudes
Do This! Don't Do That!

Verify if your home is leak-free.

Avoid flushing the toilet unnecessarily.

Take short showers.

Turn off the tap while shaving.

Turn off the tap while brushing your teeth.

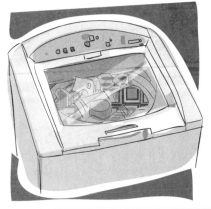

Use washing machines only when they are fully loaded.

Wash vegetables and fruit in a bowl.

8
Indians' Way of Life

hut

chief

arrow

straw hat

bowie knife

monkey

toucan

macaw

parrot

ILLUSTRATIONS: RONALDO PUCCI

Appendices

Reprodução proibida. Art.184 do Código Penal e Lei 9.610 de 19 de fevereiro de 1998.

UNIT 1 – WORD FAMILY

Adjectives	Adverbs	Translation
Group 1		
early	early	cedo; cedo
far	far	longe; longe
fast		rápido; rapidamente
	hard	difícil; dificilmente
late	late	atrasado; tarde
Group 2		
favorable	favorably	favorável; favoravelmente
gentle		gentil; gentilmente
incredible	incredibly	incrível; incrivelmente
	possibly	possível; possivelmente
probable		provável; provavelmente
simple	simply	simples; simplesmente
	terribly	terrível; terrivelmente
Group 3		
easy	easily	fácil; facilmente
	happily	feliz; felizmente
lazy	lazily	preguiçoso; preguiçosamente
lucky		sortudo; por sorte
	noisily	barulhento; ruidosamente
Group 4		
	basically	básico; basicamente
economic	economically	econômico; economicamente
dramatic		dramático; dramaticamente
ironic	ironically	irônico; ironicamente
scientific		científico; cientificamente
Group 5		
dull	dully	monótono; desanimadamente
	fully	cheio; completamente

Adjectives	Adverbs	Translation
Group 6		
due	duly	devido; devidamente
true		verdadeiro; verdadeiramente

Group 7		
good	well	bom; bem

UNIT 2 – GEO: COMBINING FORM

Combining Form	Translation
geocentric	geocêntrico
geographer	geógrafo
Geography	
geologist	geólogo
geology	
geomagnetism	geomagnetismo
Geophysics	Geofísica
geopolitics	
geothermal	geotermal

UNIT 3 – COLLOCATIONS

Collocations		Translation
	sports	fazer esportes
	a job	fazer um trabalho
Do	business	fazer negócio
	an exam	fazer um exame
	some chores	fazer algumas tarefas
	the dishes	lavar a louça
	a good impression	causar boa impressão
Make	trouble	causar problema
	an offer	fazer uma oferta
	a difference	fazer diferença
	responsibility	assumir responsabilidade
	place	realizar-se
Take	a vacation	tirar férias
	a chance	correr o risco
	advantage of something / somebody	tirar proveito de algo ou alguém

Linking Words	Translation
as soon as	tão logo que
at the end	no final
because	porque
beforehand	de antemão
by the time	quando, no momento em que
either... or	ou... ou
in advance	antecipadamente
on the other hand	por outro lado
so	então
soon	logo
when	quando
while	enquanto

UNIT 5 – AS / LIKE

Podemos utilizar *as* e *like* para dizer que algumas coisas são semelhantes.

• *Like* é uma preposição utilizada antes de substantivos ou pronomes.

> You look **like your mother**.
>
> He swims **like a fish**.

> A preposição *like* também é utilizada para dar exemplos.
>
> > She's good at languages, **like English and Spanish**.

• *As* é uma conjunção utilizada antes de uma oração e após uma expressão iniciada com preposição.

> We usually eat pizza on Saturday nights, **as many families do**.
>
> On Mondays, **as on Wednesdays**, our P.E. classes start at nine.

> Na linguagem informal, *like* é comumente utilizado no lugar de *as*.
>
> > I'm an international pilot. Nobody travels **like I do**.

> *As* também é utilizada para expressar profissões e a finalidade de objetos.
>
> > Claire has been working **as a doctor** for five years.
> >
> > Please, don't use the table **as a chair**. There's one for you here!

Adjectives	Translation
amused	divertido(a), engraçado(a)
annoyed	irritado(a)
brave	valente
capable	capaz
charming	charmoso(a)
cheerful	alegre, agradável
delightful	encantador(a)
dynamic	dinâmico(a)
enthusiastic	entusiasmado(a)
foolish	ridículo(a)
grouchy	rabugento(a)
grumpy	resmungão(gona)
helpless	indefeso(a), desamparado(a)
kind-hearted	bondoso(a)
materialistic	materialista
mean	maldoso
nasty	antipático(a)
naughty	travesso(a)
pathetic	patético(a), ridículo(a)
responsible	responsável
ruthless	impiedoso(a)
selfish	egoísta
skillful	habilidoso(a)
smiling	sorridente
snobbish	esnobe
steadfast	persistente
talented	talentoso(a)
threatening	ameaçador(a)
upset	contrariado(a), incomodado(a)
wise	sensato(a), prudente

UNIT 7 – WATER WORDS AND EXPRESSIONS

waterfalls	cachoeiras
waterless	sem água; árido(a)
waterproof	à prova d'água
water fountain	bebedouro
water-soluble	solúvel em água
water supply	reserva de água
watery	aguado(a)

UNIT 8 – PHRASAL VERBS

Phrasal Verbs	Translation
blow up	explodir
break up	terminar um relacionamento
burn up	queimar
call up	telefonar
calm down	acalmar-se
carry on	continuar uma conversa/jogo
dress up	decorar (a casa); usar roupas elegantes
get along	ter um bom relacionamento
get around	evitar alguma coisa ou alguém
get away	escapar
get by	sobreviver sem ter coisas de que você precisa ou quer
get by on	sobreviver com recursos mínimos
go into	discutir em detalhes
go on with	continuar um plano, uma conversa
go with	ter um namorado ou uma namorada; acompanhar uma pessoa
lie down	descansar; reclinar
look after	tomar conta (de uma criança, casa)
make over	fazer novamente
pass away	morrer
put away	guardar; retornar ao local apropriado
put off	adiar
put on	vestir; enganar
show up	chegar de surpresa; fazer alguém sentir-se inferior
stand by	esperar
try out	testar

Transcripts

UNIT 1. Track 2. page 17

Most teenagers around the world love junk food. But what is junk food exactly? Hamburgers, French fries, and pizza are good examples. They're bad for your health.

A healthy diet, on the other hand, includes vegetables, fruit, meat, grains, etc. – food that has vitamins and substances that are good for us.

Healthy food makes all the difference in a person's life.

UNIT 2. Track 3. page 34

The Boi-Bumbá festival brings the city of Parintins to life. 35,000 people arrive by boat and 2,000 by plane to join the two colourful troupes of characters (O Garantido and O Caprichoso) that tell the story of Amazon folklore. This atmospheric festival takes place in the Bumbódromo and there you can see a fantastic folklore spectacle created by Indians in the middle of the jungle. It is a once-in-a-lifetime privilege to assist this opera of the jungle with its costumes, beautifully dressed flag bearers, and decorated floats – all moving to the different Indian rhythms.

[...]

Extracted from <http://www.themanual2brazil.com/Destination/Manaus/Package/Parintins-Festival-by-Plane.aspx>.
Accessed on March 4, 2010.

UNIT 3. Track 5. page 54

Do you love the outdoors? Even though the Earth is a big place, every little bit you do to take care of it is important. Here are some ways people like you are volunteering:

- Clare and Lisa of Minnesota cleaned up a creek in their neighborhood and went for a swim.

- The Redwoods Class at the Prairie Creek Community School in Minnesota collected almost 60 pounds of trash near their school.

- A kindergarten class at the Village Nursery School in Massachusetts held a bake sale to raise money for the rainforest.

- A fourth grade class in New Hampshire raised salmon from eggs until they were big enough to be released into a stream.

- [...] Celina, Isabel, Julia, and Rebecca of Massachusetts cleaned up a playground in their neighborhood. First they picked up the trash. Then they hung a sign on a fence that read, "Please Keep Our Park Clean." They also had a bake sale to raise money to buy plants for their playground. [...]
- [...] Ashley and her girl scout troop in Oregon planted trees in a neighborhood park to celebrate National Arbor Day. National Arbor Day is a holiday to encourage people to plant trees. Trees produce oxygen for us to breathe, remove pollution from the air, and provide food and shelter for wildlife. [...]

Extracted from <http://pbskids.org/zoom/activities/action/way04.html>.
Accessed on February 10, 2010.

 UNIT 4. Track 7. page 70

Gandhi, the pioneer of non-violence, believed in simplicity. His simple attire became a subject of great contemplation and ridicule in Western nations. His compelling ideas braved death and continued to be a source of inspiration and emulation for great leaders like Martin Luther King Jr., Cesar Chavez, and Nelson Mandela. Here are some famous words from Gandhi.

[...]

Attitude

Be the change you want to see in the world.

Love

Whenever you are confronted with an opponent, conquer him with love.

[...]

Happiness

Happiness is when what you think, what you say, and what you do are in harmony.

Forgiveness

Hate the sin, love the sinner.

[...]

Non-violence

Non-violence is a weapon of the strong.

[...]

UNIT 5. Track 9. page 90

Located at the Newtown Cultural Precinct, Museum Africa carries a variety of exhibits, most of which pertain to the rich history of Africa. Of special interest is the display of historic works of art, which will give you an insight into artists' impressions of the Anglo-Boer War. Geological specimens, paintings, prints, photographs, and numerous objects from all corners of southern Africa are also on display. In order to fully appreciate the collection, it is best to allow at least a couple of hours for the visit.

Foundation year: 1994

UNIT 6. Track 11. page 106

From the drawing board of Brazilian cartoonist, animator, and filmmaker Mauricio de Sousa, over 200 cartoon characters for kids have come to life, led by the signature group, *Monica's Gang*. Mauricio, founder and CEO of Mauricio de Sousa Productions, the fourth-largest art studio in the world, leads a team of over 150 artists […]

Born in Santa Isabel, a small town outside of São Paulo, the son of parents who were both artists, Mauricio loved to write and draw from early on. As a young man, he moved to the big city and started out in journalism as a police reporter for the *"Folha de São Paulo"* newspaper. But his dream was to create comics. In 1959, the newspaper ran his first comic strip, starring a little blue pup named Blu. It marked the starting point for a highly successful international career that continues to expand in Brazil and around the globe.

[…]

UNIT 7. Track 13. page 126

Imagine living in a house without running water or modern washing appliances... For some this might be utopian paradise, but for most it would be a nightmare. Running water is an incredibly valuable resource with an almost endless list of applications and uses in and around the home.

The kitchen is a major consumer of water in the home, using around 10% of total household water consumption for cooking, cleaning, washing or drinking.

Of all water consumed in the home, about 15 to 20% is used in the laundry. This high utility room is a major consumer of not only water, but also energy and detergents.

The bathroom and toilet use nearly 40% of all water in the home. The shower is a water hotspot, but you can easily save water by installing a water efficient showerhead.

A slowly leaking tap can waste 20,000 liters a year. Fix it now!

[…]

Grey water is the water discharged from showers, washing machines, and dishwashers. Find out how to re-use grey water in the garden, or even set it up to flush the toilet.

[…]

Extracted from <http://www.savewater.com.au/how-to-save-water/in-the-home>.
Accessed on February 20, 2010.

UNIT 8. Track 15. page 142

Isolated indigenous peoples of Brazil

Interviewer: How many isolated indigenous groups are there in Brazil today?

Interviewed: A study carried out in 2006 pointed to the existence of 68 groups of isolated Indians.

Interviewer: Where do the isolated indigenous groups live?

Interviewed: They live in the states of Acre, Amazonas, Maranhão, Mato Grosso, Pará, Rondônia, and Roraima. There are also references to a single group living in Goiás state.

Interviewer: How do isolated indigenous groups live?

Interviewed: They hunt, fish, and collect fruits and plants. They also grow certain foods. The group photographed by the Envira River lives in six large huts and has a large cultivated area.

Interviewer: How can they stay isolated?

Interviewed: They live a semi-nomadic existence and avoid contact with other indigenous groups as well as with non-Indians. When invaders encroach on their territory they move deeper into the forest.

Interviewer: What language do isolated indigenous groups speak?

Interviewed: It is not known what language they speak. Today, 180 languages are spoken by the indigenous groups in Brazil. But it is estimated that about 1,300 were spoken at the time of the arrival of the first Portuguese colonizers in Brazil.

Extracted from <http://83.170.97.93/brazil/website/school/primary03c.pdf>.
Accessed on December 22, 2009.

Glossary

abrupt   abrupto(a)

absence   ausência

absolute   absoluto(a)

accounting   explicação

active   ativo(a)

actively   de forma ativa

activist   ativista

addicted   viciado(a)

adorable   adorável

advertiser   publicitário(a)

afraid   com medo

aftermath   período que sucede um desastre

afterwards   depois disso

against   contra

agreement   acordo

alleviation   alívio

allow   permitir

ambitious   ambicioso(a)

and   e

angry   aborrecido(a), zangado(a)

announcement   aviso

appearance   aparência

appliance   equipamento

apply   aplicar

arrange   organizar; chegar a um acordo

arrangement   arranjo; acordo

arrive   chegar

assist   ajudar, dar assistência

assistance   assistência

attempt   tentativa

attractive   atraente

await   esperar, aguardar

awful   horrível

bake sale   venda de bolos e doces para arrecadar fundos

balanced   equilibrado(a)

bargain   barganhar

bark   casca de árvore

be afraid   ter medo

be arrested   ser preso(a)

be banned   ser banido(a)

be knighted   receber título de cavaleiro

be supposed to   ter obrigação de

bed of roses   mar de rosas

before   antes

beg   implorar

behavior   comportamento

belief   crença

believe   acreditar, crer

below   abaixo

bill   lista

biodiversity   biodiversidade

biopiracy   biopirataria

blame   culpar

blossom   florescer

body   corpo

body shape   formato do corpo

boring maçante

bow reverência, mesura

brand marca

brave bravo(a), corajoso(a)

breadth amplitude, tamanho, dimensão

breath respirar

bright brilhante

burn queimar

business negócio

but mas

C

calcium cálcio

calory caloria

campaign campanha

caption legenda

car pool transporte solidário

carbohydrate carboidrato

cartoon cartum, quadrinhos

cartoonist cartunista

case caso

CEO diretor (Chief Executive Officer)

certify certificar, atestar

chapter capítulo

character personagem

cheating trapaça

child labor trabalho infantil

childhood infância

cholesterol colesterol

coach treinador(a)

co-ed (coeducational) frequentado por pessoas de ambos os sexos

color cor

community comunidade

company empresa

concern receio, preocupação

conquer conquistar

consumption consumo

cook cozinhar

cooperative que coopera

corruption corrupção

costume fantasia

courage coragem

courageous corajoso(a)

cover cobrir; capa

cowardly covarde

cream creme

create criar

cross atravessar

cross-cultural intercultural

crowded lotado(a) de pessoas

current corrente

cut cortar

D

daily diário(a)

dangerous perigoso(a)

decent decente

deceptive enganoso(a)

decline diminuir, declinar

deforestation desmatamento

defrost degelar, descongelar

demand demanda, procura

deserve merecer

desperate desesperado(a)

determined determinado(a)

different diferente

disappointed desapontado(a)

discharge descarregar

disease doença

do business fazer negócios

do the dishes lavar louça

dome   redoma

draft   rascunhar; esboço, rascunho

drain   ralo

drawing board   prancheta de desenho

dry mix   mistura em pó

E

eating disorder   distúrbio alimentar

effect   efeito

either   tampouco

emaciated   magro(a) demais, esquelético(a)

emphasize   enfatizar

employee   funcionário(a)

encroach   avançar, invadir

endangered   em perigo

endemic   endêmico(a)

energetic   com energia

energy   energia

environment   ambiente

environmental   ambiental

e-pal   correspondente na internet

exam   exame; examinar

excite   entusiasmar

excitement   entusiasmo

executioner   executor(ra)

exodus   êxodo

expect   esperar

explain   explicar

exporter   exportador(a)

exposure   exposição

extract   extrair; extrato

F

fabulous   fabuloso(a)

fact   fato

fall   cair

fat   gordura; gordo(a)

fate   destino

female   feminino(a)

fiber   fibra

fieldwork   projeto de trabalho, trabalho de campo

fight   lutar, brigar

find   achar, encontrar

find out   descobrir, encontrar

finger food   canapé

firearm   arma de fogo

flag   bandeira

flag bearer   porta-bandeira

flavor   sabor

flavored   com sabor

float   carro alegórico

flyer   folheto de propaganda

follower   seguidor(a)

fonder   mais apaixonado(a)

forced   forçado

foreigner   estrangeiro(a)

forgive   perdoar

forgiveness   perdão

foster   promover

found   fundar

founder   fundador(a)

freedom   liberdade

friendly   amigável

frightened   com medo

funny   engraçado(a)

G

garbage   lixo

generous   generoso(a)

genocide   genocídio

gifts talento
give up desistir
global warming aquecimento global
globalization globalização
good bom, boa
graduation formatura
grease gordura
greasy gorduroso(a)
greenhouse effect efeito estufa
grow cultivar
growth crescimento
guidance orientação
guide guia

hairstylist cabeleireiro(a)
happiness felicidade
happy feliz
harmful prejudicial
healing power poder curativo
healthy saudável
heartbroken triste, infeliz, de coração partido
heater aquecedor
heaven céu
helpful prestativo(a)
high standard de alto padrão
highly altamente
hilarious hilário(a)
hire contratar
homeless sem teto
honest honesto(a)
hotspot ponto chave
household chore serviço de casa
huge enorme, imenso
human rights direitos humanos
humanity humanidade

hungry com fome
hunting caça
hurt machucar

important importante
improve melhorar, aperfeiçoar
in the end por fim
include incluir
increase aumentar
indigenous indígena
infamous infame
information informação
infusion infusão
injuries maus-tratos, agressões
instant instantâneo(a)
intend pretender
interviewer entrevistador(a)

jail cadeia, prisão
jealous ciumento(a)
join juntar(-se), unir(-se)
jungle floresta

kick chutar
known conhecido(a)

launch lançar
laundry lavanderia
lawyer advogado(a)
lead levar, guiar
leaflet panfleto

leaking tap   torneira pingando

leave   sair, deixar

lecture   palestra

level   nível

library   biblioteca

lie   mentir; mentira

like   como

likely   provável

live by   viver

loathe   abominar

lock   trancar

locker   armário

look   aparência; parecer; olhar

look out for   tomar conta

lose   perder

loser   perdedor(a)

louder   mais alto(a)

loudspeaker   alto-falante

luggage   bagagem

make fun of   caçoar de, zombar de

makeup   maquiagem

malnutrition   desnutrição

martial art   arte marcial

master   dominar; mestres

mean   significar

media   meios de comunicação

medicine   medicamento

meet   encontrar

mend   consertar, remendar

messy   desarrumado(a)

migrate   migrar

minority   minoria

mirror   espelho

miss   sentir saudades; faltar

mitten   luva

mixer   mesa de som

mobilize   mobilizar

model   tomar como modelo; modelo

mortality rate   taxa de mortalidade

nervous   nervoso(a)

nightmare   pesadelo

notice   notar

novel   romance

nutrient   nutriente

nutrition   nutrição

obesity   obesidade

obligate   obrigar

obsessed   obcecado(a)

offend   ofender

oil   óleo

oily   gorduroso(a)

okra   quiabo

on behalf of   em prol de, em nome de

onion   cebola

ordinary-looking   que tem aparência normal, comum

origin   origem

orphan   órfão(ã)

outdoors   ao ar livre

over   acima de

overcrowded   superlotado(a)

overseas   importado(a)

oversee   supervisionar

overweight   acima do peso

ownership   posse, propriedade

P

package   pacote, embalagem
particular   em especial
partnership   parceria
patch   remendar
pay   pagar
pepper   pimenta
percentage   porcentagem
persuade   persuadir
physical   físico(a)
physician   médico(a), clínico(a)
placard   cartaz
plain   simples, não elaborado
playwright   dramaturgo
pleasure cruise   situação confortável
plot   enredo
policy   política
poor   pobre; fraco(a)
potassium   potássio
pound   libra (moeda/peso)
prediction   previsão
prescribe   prescrever
preserve   preservar
prevent   evitar
preventable   evitável
printed   impresso(a)
privilege   privilégio
product   produto
protein   proteína
provide   prover
publicize   anunciar
published   publicado(a)

Q

quantity   quantidade

R

raft   jangada
rainforest   floresta tropical
raise   levantar
rate   taxa
reach   alcançar
reasonable   razoável
reckless   descuidado(a)
recommend   recomendar
recover   recuperar-se
regardless   a despeito de
relative   relativo(a)
release   soltar; lançamento
renewable   renovável
respond   responder, replicar
retire   retirar; aposentar-se
reward   recompensa
ride   carona
rooted   enraizado(a)
running water   água corrente
rupee   rúpia (moeda na Índia)

S

sad   triste
salaried   assalariado(a)
salty   salgado(a)
sample   amostra, exemplo
sand   areia

satisfied   satisfeito(a)

saturated   saturado(a)

scrub forest   caatinga

search   busca

section   seção

seed   semente

self-defense   defesa pessoal

sew   costurar

shed   verter, derramar

shelter   abrigo

shores   margem, costa

shout   gritar

shrimp   camarão

sick   doente

sight   visão

silly   tolo(a)

skin   pele

skyrocketing   subindo como foguete

slave trading   tráfico de escravos

slum   favela

sociable   sociável

social worker   assistente social

sodium   sódio

soul   alma

sound   parecer; som; sonoro(a)

spend   gastar

spirited   espirituoso(a)

spread   espalhar, dispersar

staggering   impressionante

starring   estrelando

steal   roubar

store   armazenar

straight   direto(a)

stressed   estressado(a)

strong   forte

style   estilo

such as   tal como, tais como

support   apoiar

sure   claro

sureness   certeza

surf charter   expedição de surfistas

suspicion   suspeita

sustainable   sustentável

sweep   varrer

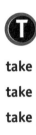

take a chance   arriscar

take care   cuidar(-se)

take place   acontecer

talk   conversar

tap   bica, torneira

taste   gosto

tasty   saboroso(a)

tattoo   tatuagem

teach   ensinar

telephone   telefone

test tube   tubo de teste

thaw   degelar, descongelar

then   então

thermometer   termômetro

threat   ameaça

through   através

timid   tímido(a)

tip   dica

title   título

torn between   dividido(a) entre duas opções

tote bag   sacola

towards   na direção de

traffic jam   engarrafamento de trânsito

trail   trilha, caminho

trash   lixo

triple   triplo

triumph   triunfo

troupe   trupe

trustworthy   confiável

truth   verdade

UFO   óvni (objeto voador não identificado)

unacceptable   inaceitável

unblock   desbloquear

unforgiving   imperdoável

union leader   líder sindical

unwilling   relutante

use   usar

vacuum   vácuo

water fountain   bebedouro

water supply   abastecimento de água

waterfall   queda-d'água

waterless   sem água

waterproof   à prova d'água

water-soluble   solúvel em água

weak   fraco(a) (p. 106)

weapon   arma

weight   peso

what matters   o que interessa ou importa

wilderness   sertão

win   vencer, ganhar

wipe out   exterminar, extinguir

wrong   errado(a)

Irregular Verbs List

Infinitive	Past	Past Participle	Translation
arise	arose	arisen	*surgir; formar-se*
babysit	babysat	babysat	*cuidar de uma criança para alguém (como babá)*
be (am/is/are)	was/were	been	*ser, estar*
become	became	become	*tornar-se, passar a ser*
begin	began	begun	*começar, iniciar*
blow	blew	blown	*soprar*
break	broke	broken	*quebrar*
bring	brought	brought	*trazer; causar*
build	built	built	*construir; formar*
burn	burnt/burned	burnt (Br)/burned (Am)	*queimar; arder*
buy	bought	bought	*comprar*
choose	chose	chosen	*escolher*
come	came	come	*vir*
cost	cost	cost	*custar*
cut	cut	cut	*cortar, partir*
do	did	done	*fazer*
draw	drew	drawn	*desenhar; planejar*
dream	dreamt/dreamed	dreamt (Br)/dreamed (Am)	*sonhar; desejar; planejar*
drink	drank	drunk	*beber*
drive	drove	driven	*dirigir, guiar; conduzir*
eat	ate	eaten	*comer*
fall	fell	fallen	*cair; baixar*
feel	felt	felt	*sentir(-se)*
fight	fought	fought	*brigar; lutar*
find	found	found	*achar, encontrar*
fly	flew	flown	*voar; pilotar*
forget	forgot	forgotten	*esquecer*
forgive	forgave	forgiven	*perdoar, desculpar*

get	got	got (Br)/gotten (Am)	*receber, obter, conseguir*
give	gave	given	*dar*
go	went	gone	*ir*
grow	grew	grown	*crescer; cultivar*
hang	hung	hung	*pendurar; suspender*
have	had	had	*ter, possuir*
hear	heard	heard	*ouvir, escutar*
hide	hid	hidden	*esconder(-se), ocultar(-se)*
hold	held	held	*prender, segurar, agarrar-se a; aguentar; sediar*
hurt	hurt	hurt	*ferir, machucar(-se)*
keep	kept	kept	*guardar; manter; permanecer; ficar; continuar*
know	knew	known	*saber; conhecer*
lead	led	led	*levar, conduzir*
learn	learned (Am)/ learnt (Br)	learned (Am)/ learnt (Br)	*aprender*
leave	left	left	*sair, deixar, partir, ir embora; abandonar*
let	let	let	*deixar, permitir*
lie	lied	lied	*mentir*
light	lit/lighted	lit/lighted	*acender(-se), iluminar, clarear*
lose	lost	lost	*perder*
make	made	made	*fazer, criar, produzir*
mean	meant	meant	*significar, querer dizer*
meet	met	met	*encontrar(-se)*
oversee	oversaw	overseen	*fiscalizar; conferir*
put	put	put	*pôr, colocar*
read	read	read	*ler*
redo	redid	redone	*refazer*
rewrite	rewrote	rewritten	*reescrever*
ring	rang	rung	*soar, tocar*
rise	rose	risen	*subir, erguer; levantar*
run	ran	run	*correr; passear; funcionar*
say	said	said	*dizer, falar*

see	saw	seen	*ver, enxergar*
seek	sought	sought	*procurar*
sell	sold	sold	*vender*
send	sent	sent	*enviar, remeter*
set	set	set	*pôr; fixar; arrumar*
sew	sewed	sewed	*costurar, remendar*
shed	shed	shed	*derramar; deixar cair; largar*
shine	shone	shone	*brilhar; iluminar; irradiar*
show	showed	showed/shown	*mostrar*
sing	sang	sung	*cantar*
sit	sat	sat	*sentar-se, estar sentado*
sleep	slept	slept	*dormir*
speak	spoke	spoken	*falar, dizer*
spend	spent	spent	*gastar*
steal	stole	stolen	*roubar, furtar*
strike	struck	struck	*golpear, atacar; acertar, atingir*
sweep	swept	swept	*varrer; arrastar*
swim	swam	swum	*nadar*
take	took	taken	*pegar, tomar*
teach	taught	taught	*ensinar, lecionar*
tear	tore	torn	*rasgar, separar; arrancar*
tell	told	told	*dizer, contar*
think	thought	thought	*pensar*
throw	threw	thrown	*lançar; atirar (algo); jogar*
understand	understood	understood	*entender, compreender*
wake	woke	woken	*acordar, despertar*
wear	wore	worn	*usar, vestir; gastar*
win	won	won	*ganhar, vencer, obter, conquistar*
withdraw	withdrew	withdrawn	*extrair, retirar, sacar; retratar(-se)*
write	wrote	written	*escrever*

Br: British English / Am: American English

Referências bibliográficas

ANTUNES, C. *A Criatividade na Sala de Aula*. São Paulo: Vozes, 2003.

_____. *As Inteligências Múltiplas e seus Estímulos*. Papirus, 1998.

_____. *Como Desenvolver Conteúdos Explorando as Inteligências Múltiplas*. Coleção "Na Sala de Aula". Fascículo 3. São Paulo: Vozes, 2001.

_____. *Como Transformar Informações em Conhecimento*. Coleção "Na Sala de Aula". Fascículo 2. São Paulo: Vozes, 2001.

_____. *O Lado Direito do Cérebro e sua Exploração em Sala de Aula*. Coleção "Na Sala de Aula". Fascículo 5. São Paulo: Vozes, 2001.

_____. *Trabalhando Habilidades, Construindo Ideias*. Coleção "Pensamento e Ação no Magistério". São Paulo: Scipione, 2001.

BAKHTIN, M. *Estética da Criação Verbal*. São Paulo: Martins Fontes, 2000.

BELMIRO, C. A. *A Imagem e suas Formas de Visualidade nos Livros Didáticos de Português*. *Educ. Soc.*, ago. 2000, v. 21, n. 72, p. 11-31.

DICIONÁRIO *Oxford Escolar para Estudantes Brasileiros de Inglês*. Oxford: Oxford University Press, 2007.

FOUCAULT, M. *A Ordem do Discurso*. 7. ed. São Paulo: Loyola, 1996.

HOLLAENDER, A. & SANDERS, S. *The Landmark Dictionary para Estudantes Brasileiros de Inglês: English/Portuguese, Portuguese/English*. São Paulo: Moderna, 2008. p. 556-557.

LONGMAN *Dictionary of Contemporary English*. 4. ed. London: Longman, 2003. p. 1259.

MACHADO, A. *A Ilusão Especular*. São Paulo: Brasiliense, 1984.

MACMILLAN *English Dictionary for Advanced Learners*. 2. ed. Oxford: MacMillan do Brasil, 2007. p. 71.

MARCUSCHI, L. A. *Produção Textual, Análise de Gêneros e Compreensão*. São Paulo: Parábola Editorial, 2008.

MURPHY, R. *Essential Grammar in Use*. Cambridge: Cambridge University Press, 2007.

ORLANDI, E. P. O Inteligível, o Interpretável e o Compreensível. In: ZIBERMAN, R.; SILVA, E. T. da (Orgs). *Leitura: Perspectivas Interdisciplinares*. 3. ed. São Paulo: Ática, 1995. p. 58-77.

Oxford Student's Dictionary of English. 7. ed. Oxford: Oxford University Press, 2001. p. 385.

PERRENOUD, P. *Construir as Competências desde a Escola*. Porto Alegre: Artmed, 1999. p. 7.

SCHNEUWLY, B. & DOLZ, J. *Gêneros Orais e Escritos na Escola*. Campinas: Mercado de Letras, 2004.

SINAI, A. et al. *Alternativas ao Aquecimento Global*. Série "Le Monde Diplomatique Brasil". São Paulo: Instituto Paulo Freire, 2007. v. 1.

SWAN, M. *Practical English Usage*. Oxford: Oxford University Press, 2005.

TORRES, C. A. et al. *Reinventando Paulo Freire no Século 21*. São Paulo: Editora e Livraria Instituto Paulo Freire, 2008. v. 1.